P9-BIT-226

CLOSET RED

A Marxist's Adventures Inside The Ruling Class

by
Bernard Livingston

WAVERLY PUBLISHERS
New York   1985

Copyright © 1985 by Bernard Livingston

First Printing 1985

Printed in the United States of America

Published by:
Waverly Publishers
235 West End Avenue
New York, N.Y. 10023

All rights reserved. No part of this book may be reproduced or
transmitted in any form or by any means, electrical or mechanical,
including photocopying, recording, or by any information storage and
retrieval system without written permission from the author, except
by a reviewer, who may quote brief passages in a review to be printed
by a magazine or newspaper, or to be broadcast via electronic media.

Library of Congress Catalog Card No. 85-51987

Livingston, Bernard, 1911—

     CLOSET RED
       1. Autobiography   I. Title.
PS

ISBN 0-961-5681-0-0 (pbk)

This book is dedicated to all those victims of U.S. Government political oppression, beginning with Tom Paine, who, after having played a major role in winning freedom for the American colonies, was rewarded by being unmercifully hounded for his radical religious opinions.

CONTENTS

Also By Bernard Livingston:

PAPA'S BURLESQUE HOUSE   *(Pyramid)*
THEIR TURF   *(Arbor House)*
ZOO: Animals, People, Places   *(Arbor House)*

CLOSET RED

Foreword

On entrance of the U.S. into World War II, the Army brass, considering that I was both a lawyer and professional photographer, felt I was uniquely qualified to be a counter-intelligence agent. Accordingly, they asked me to join the service and head a domestic anti-sabotage photographic unit.

At the time, I was a Marxist, though not a Communist Party member, and the idea of association with a U.S. Government surveillance outfit, even if it was directed against Adolph Hilter & Company, rather put me off. In any group of official gumshoes, especially those super-patriots who are enarmored of spy operations, I, a left activist, would have been a fish out of water. Commendable work, I told myself, but let them get somebody more tempermentally suited for the job.

But it was an anti-fascist war. So I finally agreed to accept the assignment. All I had to do, I felt, was soft-pedal my "red" background, so as not to arouse suspicion in my superiors, and do my part in helping to defeat the fascist enemy.

I wasn't in basic training a week before I discovered that, so far as a significant part of the army was concerned, the real enemy was here at home. A major component of my job, it turned out, was to spy on, not fascists, but so-called "reds" in the army ranks.

"Listen to what your buddies talk about," I was instructed. "Keep an eye open for communists and red propaganda, and file regular reports." This though communists were among the most ardent supporters of the war! The Cold War was being started even before the hot war had subsided.

Soon, all I could think about was getting out of this army, or, at least, out of my stool-pigeon assignment. The problem, fortunately, was solved for me well before I finished basic training. Having belatedly discovered a "red aroma" about me, my superiors concluded that I was unfit to track down nazi saboteurs. As a result I was cashiered out of the service.

What was dug up on me was never revealed, but I was certain it was my support of the democratic Spanish Republic against fascist Franco and his nazi and Italian allies. That was considered a cardinal sin by certain U.S. rulingclass circles, which hoped that communism and fascism would bleed each other white on the battlefield and leave the world to the mercy of their particular brand of capitalism.

A society inevitably reflects the values of the social class that rules it. This is as true of the U.S. as it is of the USSR. In the first instance, the values are those of the capitalist class; in the second, those of the working class. Ronald Reagan might declare that there is presently a global struggle between "communism and *democracy*." Actually, he knows that it is really a struggle between communism and *capitalism*. And, like most capitalist ideologues, he realizes that, today, capitalism's prestige in the world is rapidly diminishing. Thus, he tries to obscure the issue by substituting the word democracy for that ugly word capitalism.

It was in this context, then, that I evened the score for being prevented from doing my part as a fighter against fascism. After discharge from the army, I managed to be admitted into the world of the ruling class as an observer. There, not being suspected of sympathy with the "red focus of evil," I was able to circulate with an open eye among Kennedys, Dukes, Whitneys and other pillars of the Establishment. In the process I learned something about how, in its special style, that Establishment responds to the issues of the day.

This, then, is the substance of that excursion.

Bernard Livingston
New York City, 1985

ONE

SNOOPING AROUND AT CAMELOT

Scene I
The Castle

PROVINCETOWN, MASS., 1964—Eight months after the assassination of John F. Kennedy. The nation is still depressed; nobody exactly busting out all over.

But I am. I'm sunning myself on the P-Town beach. Every summer, for two weeks, I escape from slavery on Madison Avenue, where I toil in the ad agency mills, to this oasis of bohemianism, and try to recover from fifty weeks of unloading capitalism's consumer garbage on the American public. This year there's an additional reason for being here. P-town is close to Hyannisport. It's a good place to wait for the call that will take me to the Kennedy family compound.

How is it that I, a Marxist with no upperclass credentials at all, am being invited to so royal a preserve of the ruling class as Hyannisport? First is the fact that the Kennedys aren't aware that I'm a "red." Indeed, nobody knows it, except my family, a few close friends and comrades, and, presumably, the FBI. I'm what might be called a "closet" red—an individual who, for reasons

1

of job security, has given little public evidence that he considers U.S. imperialism humanity's chief albatross.

And since my work, successively, as lawyer, photographer, film maker, publicist and writer continually involved that very ruling class which I so decry, keeping my mouth shut has allowed access to homes which otherwise I could never dream of entering.

But there's another, more fundamental, reason why I'm being invited to the Kennedys. And that is, because of a horse, or rather, a horse movie. One day a documentary film I'd made for John Hay Whitney, during my career as film maker, came to the attention of Eunice Kennedy Shriver, the late President's sister. Fine horses are a special passion of the upper class. Eunice Kennedy Shriver's daughter, Maria, is an avid equestrienne: ergo, an invitation to screen the film to young Kennedys at the Hyannisport compound.

As a communist, closet variety or not, ordinarily I'd have as much incentive to cater to the Kennedy passion for horses, as I would to Nelson Bunker Hunt's passion for silver. But here was a chance to see how things go at Camelot. I eagerly grasped the opportunity.

"The children will be thrilled," Eunice Shriver said over the telephone. "This event should be one of the rarest pleasures of the summer. Mother will phone you at your vacation retreat to tell you the best time to drop by."

And so I sat awaiting the call from "Mother" on the P-town beach in front of the decrepit $24-a-week shack that was my "vacation retreat." Provincetown in summer is overrun by enough loonies to fill a good-sized mental ward; when I informed my landlady that President Kennedy's mother would be calling me on her phone, I could understand the indulgent look on her face. Another loony. To her the idea that the exalted Rose Kennedy would be phoning her $24-a-week tenant was as far-fetched as the idea, forty years ago, that a certain lace-curtain Boston Irishman (at the moment grounded in a wheelchair at Hyannisport) would sire a U.S. President and two senators besides.

"Mr. Livingston! President Kennedy's mother is on the phone!" the landlady screams from her porch two days later—loud enough for all Provincetown to hear. Deliberately she uses the words *President Kennedy's mother*, not *Mrs. Kennedy*, so that her neighbors will damn well know who's on *her* phone.

In eight seconds flat I'm off the beach and in the house with phone in hand. "Yes, Mrs. Kennedy . . ."

"I don't know why Eunice sets up these things without letting me know . . ." There's a note of annoyance in her voice: the irritation of a mother bugged by pranks of an hyperactive child. "The children stare their eyes out all week on movies. To say nothing of TV . . ."

Uh-aw, don't tell me the Dowager Queen is going to wash my trip to Camelot down the drain.

"But this is something special, Mrs. Kennedy," I stutter anxiously. "It's an educational movie."

"Educational?"

"It's a film about the life of a thoroughbred horse . . ."

"Horse? Did Jackie have anything to do with this?"

"No, not Jackie. Mrs. Shriver set it up. But the film deals with much more than the life of a thoroughbred. There are marvelous breeding and birth scenes. The children will learn something about the wonder of procreation."

3

"You mean it's a *sex* film?" Her voice leaps a full octave.

"No, Mrs. Kennedy, you wouldn't exactly call it a sex film. It's about birth and life as told through the career of a racehorse."

"As if we already don't have enough problems with the children! Letting them see such things! Does Eunice know exactly what's in this film?"

"I'm not sure. I never thought to ask her. But what she does know is that it won several awards as an educational film. And that it was sponsored by John Hay Whitney who, like your husband, was once Ambassador to Great Britain." (I'm now using whatever leverage I can.)

"Well, Eunice asked you to come. So I guess you'd better. Get here by noon and you can have lunch."

Nine children of her own and an army of grandchildren, yet still reluctant to let them learn about the facts of life! Oh well, a Kennedy is a Kennedy is a Kennedy. The lady is a devout Catholic. And, except for the quantity of offspring and the exalted station, I guess she's no different from my own Jewish mother who still tells her grandchildren the stork brought them here.

By noon I'm pulling up in a taxi to the gates of Camelot. I'm loaded down with two heavy cans of film. (No burdensome movie projector to carry, thank God; the Hyannisport compound has, naturally, its private movie theater.) It's the peak of July. I'm pouring sweat, dressed as I am in a Dunhill navy blazer, white flannel slacks, blue silk shirt and tie, which I've bought

4

specially for the visit to the Castle. I feel like poor Scott Fitzgerald acting out his compulsion to mix with the very rich.

At the gate a guard stops me. Oh Jesus, Secret Service! It's only a few months since the assassination. Oswald, Russia, Castro—the Feds are gung-ho about "radicals." What if they have a copy of my FBI file in this guardpost?

Either I'm not important enough a "red," or my elegant Scott Fitzgerald outfit assures them that I harbor no malevolence against the rich. Either that, or J. Edgar Hoover has once again bungled national security, for, after a phone call to somewhere, my FBI file doesn't turn up, and the sentries pass my taxi through.

Whizzing down the lane toward the main house, that rambling old wooden mansion that was the late President's summer White House, I'm thinking about my Dunhill jacket. Apart from the fact that it has set me back $250, a price I can ill afford, I'm beginning to feel there's something obscene about my going to the class enemy's palace dressed like a nobleman. Moreover, in the July heat, my sweat has already soiled the jacket down to a quarter of its purchase price.

Oh well, Lenin travelled home to the Revolution in a sealed train, courtesy of his class enemy, the German High Command. (Of course, he was a known Bolshevik, useful to the Germans for withdrawing Kerensky's Russia from the war, and I, only a closet communist, who will show some capitalist young Kennedys a movie about a thoroughbred horse.) So who am I to complain?

The taxi passes a Quonset-roofed swimming pool. The water seems to be heated, steam rises from its surface. Can this be for use of the ailing Old Man? Looking back from the taxi, I catch a glimpse of the wheel-chaired Ambassador peering out of a second-story window, as though keeping an individual Kennedy surveillance on subversive intruders.

A few hundred more yards and I'm there. The house that JFK vacationed in! Summer seat of the Fabled Family! I've entered Camelot, not in my usual role as hired hand, but as invited guest: an artist "commanded" to show his work to the Reigning Dynasty. Wait till my subversive friends back in New York hear about this!

At the door a rosy-cheeked Irish domestic greets me. I'm to make myself comfortable in the parlor, Mrs. Shriver will be over shortly. I find myself a chair and sit. It has been some time now since JFK has been in this house, but you can still feel the Kennedy Presence. Movement, action, thrust. People barge in and out. Doors open and close. In a corner of the room there are two infants in separate playpens (which future senators are these?). They vigorously try to strike each other with plastic rattles, already in training, it seems, for those future touch-football games.

So this is Camelot. Well, at least there's relief from the July heat in this splendid old clapboard mansion. But those paintings on the walls, my God! Atrocious! Limegreen, sea-sailing scenes that look like oversize Woolworth prints. Where are the Matisses and Manets associated with Jackie? Who selected these cliches for the President's summer residence? It couldn't have been Jacqueline Kennedy—whatever else one might say, she has style. Could this be the one place where JFK indulged his lockerroom tastes?

I look out the window. Children with nannies all over the shamrock-green grass. Pregnant young women dot the landscape, hurrying here and there. You get a feeling you're in a baby-making plant that's on a 24-hour shift. Nobody moves slowly. Everybody except the uniformed nannies is in beach shorts and T-shirts. I'm beginning to feel, in my soggy Scott Fitzgerald costume, like some uniformed lackey myself.

The front door flies open and a jaunty highly-tanned man leaps inside. "Hullo," he pipes, extending a hurried hand, "I'm Petah Lawfod."

With that accent, who else?

"Eunice will be over in a moment. Can I get you a drink or something?"

"Thanks. Vodka and tonic would be fine." I watch the Kennedy clan's delegate to the Rat Pack throw together the drink as neatly as he does it for Frankie at Las Vegas.

"Eunice is up with the Old Man," says Peter, thrusting the concoction at me. "Needs lots of attention. She's his pet, and there are some things he'll permit only Eunice to do for him. She'll be by presently." And he's up and out faster than Sammy Davis, Jr. can do a time step.

Hardly has the wind of Peter Lawford's exit eddied down when a second hurricane comes swushing up to the door. Bobby and Teddy: the two luminaries of the clan, now that Jack is gone. You get the feeling that each is dying to get through that door ahead of the other. Somewhere I'd read that Jacqueline Kennedy's first glimpse of the family's competitive spirit came when she saw a five-year-old Kennedy push a four-year-old Kennedy who, in turn, immediately shoved a three-year-old Kennedy. You can sense this kind of combativeness in the Hyannisport air. Those two infant quarterbacks striking their plastic rattles at each other in the playpens across the room were already adding up their points. Yet, this *is* Camelot, and sibling rivalry must yield to primogeniture: Bobby, despite his puny size, pops through the door ahead of the larger Teddy.

I am now in the joint presence of a U.S. Attorney General and a U.S. Senator. And even though I feel that the one is a quick-change artist who, for career reasons, had jilted witch-hunting Joe McCarthy to woo "red" Dr. King, and the other a hot-shot who cribbed through Harvard and wouldn't have been elected dogcatcher were he not a Kennedy, I am momentarily mesmerized. Swept off my feet. Kennedyized. For a moment, forgetting who I am, there's a fantasy of being accepted as a buddy into the sweet intimacies of this beautiful, honeyed, mon-eyed, rulingclass world!

What makes so-called democratic human beings so ful-somely adore "royalty?" How come one little game of touch football can turn left-leaning Jack Newfield into seeing the McCarthyite Bobby Kennedy as a re-born populist hero? What social malaise drives wealthy-in-his-own-right Truman Capote to sell his soul as court jester to the super-rich?

"You the fellow with the movie?" asks Ted Kennedy, all tan and ivory-toothed in a summer business suit. (I'm still locked into my straightjacket of a court costume.).

"Yes, Livingston, Bernard Livingston. I . . ."

"I'm Ted Kennedy. This is Bobby . . ."

"Hi," grunts Bobby, his eyes glued to the magazine he's thumbing through.

"Eunice will be over shortly," says Ted. "Sorry Bobby and I can't stay to see your movie. We've got to rush down to Washington."

"Oh, that's okay. But why do you Kennedys rush about so?" I ask, trying to ingratiate myself with sparkling wit.

"Do we rush?" intercepts Bobby, in perfect seriousness. "I thought we simply moved faster than most people."

I laugh artificially, like a comic who has failed to get a laugh from his audience.

"It's a shame Jackie can't be here," says Ted. "She loves horses. But she's up at Newport with her family."

A servant comes into the room, wheeling a service of food, and leaves.

"Have yourself some lunch," says Ted. The two brothers sample snacks from the service tray, chewing them with vigor. At the sound of an automobile horn outside, both canter quickly to the door.

"Bye," says Bobby.

"Bye," echoes Ted.

The Attorney General gets through the door first.

Have yourself some lunch. Okay, better have some food while I can. Who knows—maybe I'll be shanghaied into a touch football game *before* lunch. I examine the tray of tiny sandwiches at which the brothers have picked. Watercress! Paper-thin sandwiches of watercress on white bread, layered with a smidgin of egg salad! This is *lunch*? This why the clan always looks so Spartanly slim? Oh, Jackie, where is your renowned *cordon bleu*?

As I sit there nibbling my watercress and thumbing through

Maria Montessori's *Method*, picked up from a coffee table, another comet comes streaking through the door. Eunice at last! I can tell it's Eunice Kennedy Shriver—the hairdo a reddish-brown horse's mane, the face a fine-boned, high-cheeked Katharine Hepburn. Figure lean, athletic and power-packed. It all unmistakably adds up to a photo I've seen in *Vogue*.

"So sorry to keep you waiting," she declaims in a take-charge voice which assures you that, were she not a woman, *this* would be the next President Kennedy. "But Dad is sometimes a problem. Occasionally he needs special attention."

"So Mr. Lawford told me. But there was no need to rush. I didn't mind waiting."

"You've had lunch?"

"Yes."

"Something to drink?"

"Oh, yes. First thing, courtesy of Mr. Lawford. This copy of Maria Montessori here," I say, picking up the book. "From what I've heard of your interest in child education, especially your work with the mentally retarded, I'll wager it's yours, right?"

"Yes. It's difficult enough bringing up the normal child, let alone the handicapped. Montessori is an enormous help."

"Absolutely. And I'd think Montessori would be the first to G-rate my Whitney horse film. But your mother seemed to feel it should be X-rated. It has scenes of horses copulating and a sequence on birth."

"Oh my!" Eunice gasps. "I hadn't realized. I was simply told it was a marvelous film about horses."

"But that's just it, Mrs. Shriver. What *makes* it marvelous is that it *has* these scenes. Kids adore horses, and Montessori would certainly agree that the best way to teach them the facts of life is not via the birds and bees but rather by way of something all kids love: horses."

"We've enough problems with the facts of life as it is. Haven't you a less explicit film?"

"But why rush children to adulthood uninformed?"

That remark provokes the Kennedy royal ire; for a moment Eunice Kennedy Shriver fixes me with those regal eyes. *Buddy boy*, they say, *my parents didn't do too badly with the children they rushed to adulthood, did they now? Nor Ethel and Bobby, nor Sarge and myself.* "The children would be disappointed if they didn't see some kind of horse movie. You *must* have something else."

"Well, if you insist," I reply, picking up my two heavy cans of film. "Yes, I do. I also brought along *The Maryland Horse*. Quite innocuous. Lots of horse show stuff in it. Jumping, exhibiting, equitation . . ."

"Oh, fine. Come, let's go. The kids are waiting in the theatre." Over my chivalric protest, she grabs the two heavy cans of film to carry them herself. And out the door we go, myself bringing up the rear. A Kennedy is a Kennedy is a Kennedy: first in war, first in peace . . . first out the door.

Scene 2
Flashback to:

HORIZON HOUSE—a live-in therapeutic community in New York City for teenage drug addicts struggling to return to a drug-free life. A black house, painted black for reasons of economy. It's 1968, four years after my visit to the white house in Hyannisport. My friend Pedro, an ex-addict, teaches at Horizon House and has invited me to show the Whitney film to the kids. Junkies. An American Tragedy—boys and girls, twelve years old and up, from broken ghetto homes. Most have never seen a real live horse except the mounted cop's.

In the film they see the young Whitney jockey: rich, famous, laid-back. Strong tiny hands mastering a powerful animal, a hero. They fantasize, projecting their own miserable lives into the movie. The birth of the little foal: horsechild cherished by a protecting mother. They witness the drama of parturition in all its frightening detail. Breathless silence. They wonder, dream some more.

Now the film flashes back to fundamentals. No birds and bees. Rather, a penis, a vagina, a mating scene, orgasm, semen, even the veterinarian's test pictures of sperm cells wriggling in the seminal fluid. Whispers, nervous giggles. *Lights! Lights!*

"Lights! Stop the film!" yells the director of Horizon House.

I turn the projector off. Lights go on.

"Who snickered?" demands the ex-addict director, a tough, big-brother figure. "Raise your hands."

Several hands are lifted, including that of an undernourished teenage boy who wears a sandwich sign: I SWIPED FROM MY BROTHERS AND SISTERS. I'M TRULY SORRY.

"Apologize to Mr. Livingston," orders the director.

"No, no," I protest. "There's no offense."

"That's not it," he says, addressing himself to his charges. "This man has been good enough to come here and teach you something you should learn not in a shithouse or back alley, but in a decent setting. And you snicker. Apologize!"

Dead quiet—serious attentive silence—for the remainder of the film, which shows the well-loved foal leaving its mother to go on to racing glory. In the discussion following: questions, deep and touching questions.

"Do all mother horses love their babies like that?" a scrawny, sad-faced girl asks.

"Good question," I reply. "No, not always. One mare that I filmed tried to stamp her newborn baby to death. Know why? Because it was her first baby and a difficult birth gave her terrible pain. They gave the baby to a foster mother. But you know something? After the real mother got over the pain they gave her back her baby. And she loved it ever after." The scrawny sad-faced girl clasps her hands with joy. I can see the lump rising in her throat.

"Why are you so tough on them?" I ask the director after the session is over.

"That's what they respect. Toughness. These are junkie kids. Never had parents worth the name. But somehow they know that a good parent is tough as well as tolerant."

Now *there*, by God, is a parent for you! Not afraid of the facts of life. Knows how to put on a real family show. Would even get my vote for President of the U.S.A.

Scene 3
Dissolve back to:

THE KENNEDY PRIVATE THEATRE AT THE HYANNISPORT COMPOUND. The audience, mostly Kennedy teenagers and their friends, find little to snicker at in the screening of my sanitized sexless *Maryland Horse*. They've grown up with the equitation, showing and dressage the film depicts. The screening is a flop. The older Kennedy boys can't wait to beat it into Hyannis Village to puff joints and crack shithouse jokes about the facts of life.

And I can't wait to leave the scene where I've laid so miserable an egg, although it has taught me a thing or two about the so-called sophistication of our premier rulingclass clan. I get into the limousine that Eunice Shriver has assigned to transport me back to Provincetown. My chauffeur is Bobby Kennedy's assistant athletic director.

"That's right," the crew-cut, military-looking young man assures me as he speeds up Route Six. "Assistant athletic director. Each family has its own athletic director. Kennedys can get ulcers if they lose a contest. Especially if they lose to each other."

"But *assistant* athletic director . . . you mean each family has a head director too?"

"Bobby's family makes almost a whole football team by itself. He insists on a chief and an assistant. He's the most aggressive, toughest and ruthless of the clan. Everybody starts polishing doorknobs when they know Bobby's on the way up here."

"I always thought it was the Old Man who ran the show."

"I'm talking about rivalry between the sons and daughters. Sure, the Old Man calls the tunes, even now as a wheelchair case. Remember when Harry Truman said he was more afraid of Pop than the Pope if Jack became President? Well, now I know what he meant. Once, walking past the study in the big house, I overheard the Old Man chewing Jack out for something he did as President without first consulting him. Can you imagine anybody rubbing a President's nose in it like he was a naughty dog? And the President of the United States just sat there and took it with his tail between his legs. The Old Man's like a Mafia don in his family. He orders them all around and nobody, not even the President, crosses him."

TWO

Trojan Horse in the Royal Court of the Whitneys

1.

It's 1949, and I'm living on Park Avenue in an apartment with rent appropriate to a member of the ruling class. But I haven't a cent to my name. It's the period of my poverty as an impecunious film maker, long before I became a well-paid wage-slave on Madison Avenue. My wife (no Pollyanna) is bitching about having to make soybean mash taste like steak. Con Edison will be arriving any day to cut off the utilities. I'm trying to discover how I can tap the landlord's electrical outlet in the hall-way.

How, I keep asking myself, do you go about raising money on a mere idea? Because ideas are the only equity I have, unless I want to hock my cameras. Where would a film maker get a commission to produce an epic that would bring him fame and fortune—or, for the moment, simply fortune?

"Jock Whitney," volunteers my wife as, muttering out loud, I pace past the kitchen.

"Who?"

"John Hay Whitney," she replies, looking dourly at the soybean mash she's padding into "hamburger" patties. "And soon, please God. I'm running out of ways to transform the lowly soybean into meat."

"What do you mean, John Hay Whitney? He's one of the richest men in the world. Why would he finance a film by a red like me?"

"Look, you've been querying the air for the last five days: 'Who can I get to finance a film?' I'm telling you Jock Whitney."

"Why would Jock Whitney all of a sudden want to finance a film?"

"Because he financed *Gone With the Wind* for David Selznick. Because he put up the money for Billy Rose's *Jumbo*. Because he underwrote *Life With Father*. Because he's angelled just about everything from technicolor to Minute Maid Orange Juice. Jock Whitney just loves putting up millions for things, especially films. Don't you ever read the gossip columns?"

"But I'm a communist, not David Selznick, not Technicolor and certainly, thank God, not Billy Rose."

"No, you're an idiot. Doesn't Jock Whitney own a thoroughbred farm? Isn't horseracing as dear to him as his very own 'thoroughbred' mother? Don't you know how these human thoroughbreds feel about their grand old sport? If you don't, I do."

"So what?"

"So Jock Whitney would be a sitting duck to angel a film about his great passion, that's what. How'd you like your sawdust hamburgers tonight? With that ketchup I swiped at the Automat, or the mustard I lifted from Bickford's?"

I had about as much access to John Hay Whitney as I had to the Llama of Tibet. And getting his ear was as easy as climbing an Himalaya; the man had more secretaries than a U.S. President, more hideaways than Howard Hughes. I knew this because, in order to arrange a five-second head shot of Mr. Whitney for a movie I'd just produced for the exclusive U.S. Jockey Club, of which he was a steward, I had to pursue him (by phone) to all of his eight palazzos around the world. For, despite the chummy moniker, "Jock," this elusive aristocrat went extremely low profile, especially outside his own social class. Only because I was making the film for the Jockey Club, did I finally succeed in capturing him. And I was certain that he forgot about me faster than it took to shoot his five-second headshot.

Nevertheless, since I was desperate—convinced that I would soon sprout soybeans in my ears—my wife's suggestion of an epic film on the thoroughbred, a kind of equine *Gone With the Wind* angelled by the backer of the real GWTW, sounded like a great idea. A drowning man grasps at any straw.

How to reach that straw? A phone call to J.H. Whitney & Co. would get me Mrs. Hill, the charming, patrician lady secretary who blocks off access to the Boss like a hockey goalie blocks a punt. Trying his "Buckingham Palace" in Manhasset or any of his other regional seats would only invite: "Mr. Whitney is not here at the moment, sir, may I have your name?" And a letter outlining so ambitious a project as I had in mind would undoubtedly go unanswered, or at least take six months to elicit the inevitable rejection. The straw seemed, at the moment, to be floating on the far side of the Atlantic.

In desperation I turn to the *Racing Form*. A match race, I notice in its news column, is to be run on Saturday between Calumet Farm's Coaltown and John Hay Whitney's Capot at

Pimlico Racetrack in Baltimore.

"By God, I've got it! By God, I've got it!" I exclaim, sounding like Rex Harrison in *My Fair Lady*.

"You mean we're going to Twenty-One Club for dinner tonight?" my wife chirps, noting the ecstatic expression on my face.

"Not tonight, baby, but soon. Jock Whitney has Greentree Stable, that is, Capot in a match at Pimlico Saturday. Pimlico doesn't make patrol movies of each race as Belmont Racetrack does. So I'll shoot the race myself. If Capot wins I'll have the only film of the event. That horse is dear to Whitney's heart, and if Capot beats Coaltown I'll have this top dog of the ruling class by the balls. At least I'm certain the film will give me a chance to get his ear."

"Machiavelli, you! Hatching such sneaky plots. But what are you going to use for money? Train fare isn't free, hotels charge for rooms and Eastman Kodak wants cash on the barrel head for film."

"I'll send Henry down to Pimlico to shoot the film. He bills me per diem and lays out all expenses from his own pocket."

"And if Capot doesn't win?"

"I'll find a new career. Grow soybeans maybe."

Meantime I stay up all night working on an outline of the epic film I want to make. It will be the definitive film on the thoroughbred horse, that most noble of nature's creatures. Through Capot it will tell the story of the fiery desert steed, which came to England from Arabia in the 18th century and mated with the common English mare to produce a line of thoroughbreds that has enchanted the upper class ever since, from

Eclipse to Man O'War. With scenes of mating and birth shown for the first time on color film, the movie will be both a landmark film documentary and an allegory of life. (This, incidentally, although I don't know it at the moment, is the film that later will bring about that visit to Hyannisport.)

It's cold and blustery down at Pimlico the day of the match race. The sky is threateningly dark. The race could easily be snowed out. With a stallion like Capot worth a fortune on the breeding farm, Jock Whitney could cancel at the last minute for fear of injury to his horse. Or those ominous clouds might open up and wash out the possibility of shooting a screenable film. Worse still, Calumet's Coaltown might run Whitney's Capot into the ground and shaft my whole damn plan.

Fortunately none of these disasters occur. Capot lopes across the finish line one-and-a-half lengths ahead of the sorely-punished Coaltown, and I, listening to the radio broadcast in New York while Henry shoots the race at Pimlico, leap in the air like one of those New Jersey barbers who are always winning the New York Lottery.

"We *do* go to Twenty-One Club tonight, don't we?" concludes my wife with a feline smile on her face.

"You betcha life, baby!" I exclaim. "Even if we have to pawn your stock of soybeans!"

The following week, after Henry returns with the film and I stall his request for payment with promises of a part in the upcoming movie epic, I carefully edit the footage. In it, John Hay Whitney, owner, with his sister, Joan Whitney Payson, of Greentree Stable and a sizeable chunk of the rest of the universe, is in the Pimlico winner's circle accepting the victory cup. He's happy as a boy with his first Erector set, and turns the trophy over to his trainer to be mounted along with other prizes in his museum of personal triumphs. The first leg of my Machiavellian plot has been implemented.

Now to the next leg. I package the five-minute reel of film, which thus far has cost me only a promissory note to Henry for his expenses. (Henry is a rich young dilettante so anxious to break into film-making that, despite his fear of horses, he is willing to mortgage his bank account to work on the planned Whitney movie.) I place the Capot film in a shipping container along with a print of my just-completed Jockey Club movie and attach a prestigious-looking label: BERNARD LIVINGSTON PRODUCTIONS. Then I insert in the package the next bet in my Machiavellian parlay: a letter which reads:

> Dear Mr. Whitney,
>   We enclose for your personal approval, before release, a print of the film which we recently completed for the Jockey Club, in which you are shown as one of its stewards.

(Actually, of course, this is merely a ploy, for I no more need his approval of his five-second head shot than the jackal requires the lion's approval to scavenge the leftovers).

> In addition we include some footage we shot on Capot winning the Pimlico Special while our crew [*crew! one man—Henry*] was working on another project at the racetrack. The footage is of course of no special importance to us but we thought you might like seeing it.
>   Also we are sending along a presentation which embodies an idea for a personal film project that we feel might be of interest to you. We hope you will find an opportunity to glance through

the enclosed film outline and we are certainly anxious to hear
your reactions to it.

Sincerely,
Bernard Livingston Productions
Bernard Livingston, Director

The time-bomb fully assembled, I invest ten dollars of my
fast dwindling cash reserves to deliver it by special messenger to
the seat of the Whitney empire on the 32nd floor of the International Building in Rockefeller Center.

Five days pass. Nearing Christmas. The big Vermont pine
tree in Rockefeller Center has been blinking Yuletide cheer night
after night; mock angels ensconced on the front of Saks Fifth
Avenue are carolling round-the-clock blessings; St. Patrick's
Cathedral overflows with tourists bearing gifts. But nothing for
me. I prowl obsessively around Rockefeller Center to look up at
a certain 32nd floor window, fantasizing that a letter will come
hurtling down to me in some imaginary chute, the way cash once
travelled through tubes in department stores.

"Where were you?" my wife growls as I come in from the
bitter cold. "Mrs. Hill called to ask if it was all right for Mr.
Whitney to keep the Capot film over the Christmas holidays. He
wants his kids to see it when they get home from school."

"Jock Whitney called to ask a favor of *me*? Yipes!" I
exclaim, doing a victory jig like Hitler in the Compiegne Forest.
"I hope you told Mrs. Hill okay."

"*Our* Christmas is grim enough. Would I spoil it for those
poor deprived Whitney urchins? Of course I told her to keep it."

"It looks like we're in baby! We've leaped the first hurdle and we're out in front!"

New Year's Eve arrives. Henry, already envisioning his name on a list of film credits, stakes us to a gala champagne dinner. We go to the Twenty-One Club to mix with the upper crust. Topping the evening, as we exit, tipsy with bubbly, we get ourselves photographed like Scott and Zelda astride the plaster jockeys that line Twenty-One's snooty steps. The good cheer is enough to carry me over to the next day.

Later that next day, coming home from the public library, where, optimistically, I am already doing research for the proposed film, I encounter my wife's grim face.

"What's the matter?" I inquire. "Still feeling last night's binge?"

"It's fallen through," she moans.

"Wha-what's fallen through?" I stutter, holding my stomach which suddenly goes nauseous.

"Mrs. Hill just this minute called to ask where she should return the film. I told her here. She was about to hang up, when I asked, 'What about Mr. Livingston's movie proposal?' 'Oh,' she replied ever so sweetly, 'Mr. Whitney thought it was ever so interesting. But he isn't planning anything like that at the moment. You'll probably be getting a note from him soon.' "

Without waiting to shout curses, I grab my hat and dash out the door. This time I head not for the public library but for the corner saloon.

"Where were you?" my wife bellows on my return six martinis later—a superfluous question considering my obvious condition. "You're never here when you should be. Jock Whitney called!"

"Whitney called?" I burp. "Hisselv'?"

"Yes, himself! He wants you in his office ten a.m. tomorrow!"

"Me? Wassa mattah, Jock Whitney can' naffor' tuh messinger th' film back tuh me? I godda pickit up myselv'?"

"No, idiot! He said there'd been a foulup in communication. Mrs. Hill was supposed to ask about returning the film, yes. But she was also to tell you he wanted to discuss your movie proposal."

"Wassa mattah? The president of Whitney Worldwide Communications can' neven communicate with hizz zeckatary? Wassa mattah?" The truth, of course, was that, although drunk, I was ecstatic not belligerent.

The next morning, an unexpectedly bright one, considering my drunken binge of the night before, I'm sitting in the office of John Hay Whitney. The fabulous "Jock," blueblood "angel" of Wall Street, Broadway and Hollywood, star of polo and high finance, scion who inherited the largest personal fortune ever probated up to 1927 ($239,301,017 in 1927 dollars) only to triple it again before he reached fifty. Here is a capitalist nabob whose houseguests are kings and presidents, whose signature on checks is sought by the David Selznicks, the Billy Roses, the Michael Todds . . . And he has asked *me*, a closet communist who hasn't $2.39 in his pocket, to call at his private office to discuss the movie production of *Greentree Thoroughbred*!

The prospect terrifies me. Why had I thrust myself onto

this frightening stage? Had I the talent to deliver a performance that would win the approval of a man accustomed to dealing with the world's top professionals? Or would I be booed off the boards for the gross amateur I would inevitably reveal myself to be? And what if, in this most capitalist of all worlds, my political orientation is discovered? Beads of sweat moisten the copy of the film outline I hold in my hands.

"I like what you did with the Jockey Club movie," allows His Majesty, surrounded by wallsful of testimonials to his indulgences in the lively arts (all of course at a princely profit). "And I was especially pleased with that little film of Capot winning the Pimlico Special."

"We felt that Capot's unique talent should not go unrecorded for future generations as happened with Pavlova and Nijinski." (Uh-aw, watch it! Stay away from things Russian, even *white* Russian).

"This movie outline—do you think you can implement on film what you do with words?"

"If you *liked* the Jockey Club film, sir, you will *love* Greentree Thoroughbred. I guarantee that."

"And you have a solid production company, a competent crew, good cameramen?"

"The best." (Not a gross lie, really, since even though *I* am actually the entire company, crew and camera staff, I certainly consider myself the best).

"What about the soundtrack?"

"Again the best. We'll take our musical score from Mozart. He was a born film composer and his music is in the public domain."

"Well, I guess there's nothing left but to get to work, is there?" The Emperor presses a button. "Ask Mr. Park to come in," he orders a fourth assistant to Mrs. Hill as she responds to the call.

Twenty minutes later I walk out of the International Building with a contract signed by Samuel C. Park, who is president of the Whitney thoroughbred horse subsidiary, Greentree Stud, Inc. In my pocket is a check for the largest amount I've ever dreamed of. I feel like Michelangelo with his papal commission for decoration of the Sistine Chapel. I also feel like one of the Hollywood Ten who has been assigned to direct a film for communist-hating Louis B. Mayer.

2.

The mating of thoroughbreds, particularly on an upperclass horse farm as royal as John Hay Whitney's Greentree Stud, is an exercise in elitism equalling only that of the class which owns them. In the joinder of two elite thoroughbred horses, there's as much concern for matching pure bloodlines, for obtaining strategic family advantage and for assuring production of acceptable heirs, as there was in the linking of two imperial houses in 18th century Europe.

In a way, the mating of their thoroughbreds serves as a symbolic sharing of class values between aristocratic horse owners that is often more highly regarded than mutual membership in the various elite clubs they patronize. The *nouveau riche* can occasionally wangle membership in the elite clubs. But none but a select rulingclass group ever gets a stud service to a horse such as Secretariat or his kind.

And the mating of two such thoroughbreds is the spectacle that I am to film for the edification of posterity in the documentary movie, *Greentree Thoroughbred*. Ampitheater, one of the thoroughbred "Princes" that help preserve the royal bloodlines at Greentree, has been selected as star of the film. His co-star is the mare, "Princess" Begum, owned by the Aga Khan.

The day before, to determine if she was in season, the mare had been "teased." This is a procedure in which a non-thoroughbred stallion, the "teaser"—a kind of lowerclass "bum" unworthy of mating with thoroughbreds—is allowed to nuzzle the Princess (with a fence between them to prevent sexual consummation). Teasing by a worthless half-bred is done to avoid burdening the thoroughbred Prince, who can't afford to waste his precious libido on a lot of useless fooling around. If the Princess responds to the bum's advances by kicking, it means she's not interested in sex, no matter what the social status of the suitor. If she returns his nuzzling, then she's willing, and having no class prejudice, would gladly allow the bum into her bed.

No such thing, however, would ever take place. If the Princess shows interest, the bum is dismissed and she is led to the court of the thoroughbred Prince. Like an official taster who pre-tests the monarch's food, the bum simply stands by until called to render service at the next royal nuzzling.

Prince Ampitheater, as with most of the male sex, is of course always willing. For this reason, lest he go berserk with passion, he is kept away from the mare until she has been made ready for actual mating. For her, this means having her snout fitted with a restraining "twitch," and her legs hobbled to prevent kicking or otherwise injuring the stallion. In addition, a half-dozen strong men help keep her in receiving position. She looks about as pleased as a female slave manacled for a bondage orgy with some dissolute Byzantine pasha.

Now Ampitheater is brought up from his barn. Sighting the mare, he instantly produces an erect penis. A groom, controlling the stallion with a long rein, allows him to approach the hobbled mare and sniff her scent, which causes his neck to arch magnificently and his warhorse body to gleam with the sweat of his lust. As he is reined back from the mare, he signals his impatience by rearing on his hindlegs and opening his lips to show his teeth: Alexander the Great's Bucephalus about to charge!

Now in the fullness of potency, kicking and protesting, he has his eighteen inch-long penis washed with antiseptic by a groom. The half-dozen strong men then move in to take hold of the mare, and the veterinarian alerts himself for action. During all this I am weaving in, out and under with hand camera for closeups. Henry, somewhat frightened by proximity to the fiery stallion, films the scene at longshot distance.

Foreplay between the two animals having been reduced to only that necessary for the stallion's erection, and preliminary amenities over—including antisepticizing the mare's genitals— Ampitheater is now unreined. He mounts the mare, with a groom directing his penis into her vagina; she responds by trying to kick, despite the hobbles. One of the strong men tightens the twitch on her snout; the others push her back to the stallion, who nips possessively at her neck. The stallion pumps and pumps, the mare withdraws and withdraws, while each time the strong men force her back. In a moment the reason for the whole Keystone Komedy is over: Prince Ampitheater has reached orgasm, ejaculated his precious million-dollar sperm into Princess Begum and quietly backs off.

Here the veterinarian gives nature an assist. To assure conception he takes a sample of semen from the stallion's dripping penis, seals it in a capsule, and, with a rubber-gloved hand, shoves the capsule into the mare's vagina. The female breeding-machine, which, as a racehorse, had won its master the world-famous English Oaks, is then released from bondage and walked back to her stall. As she passes a nearby paddock, a certain lower-class bum of no worth for thoroughbred breeding, stops his grazing, rushes up to the fence and, rearing up, displays his decaying teeth in a fit of sexual passion. He might just as well have saved himself the trouble.

"What's the rationale for this depressing spectacle?" I ask the vet as I film him examining a sampling of Ampitheater's sperm under the microscope. "Thoroughbred racing is called the sport of kings. This man-managed rape hardly seems kingly and certainly not sporting. At least not for the mare and the teaser."

"I see you're an idealist," he replies. "The breeding end of this game is not a sport, fellow. It's a business. That's what delivers the big money."

"Okay. But why not simply turn the mare loose at pasture with the stallion and let nature take its course. I'll wager you'd get better foals."

"Maybe. But you wouldn't get as many. Pasture breeding yields about 50-percent pregnancies, controlled breeding up to 85-percent. On a big farm that 35-percent difference makes an enormous difference in dollars."

"Why not use artificial insemination, then? Think of all the stud services you could get from just one stallion."

"Wouldn't do. A thoroughbred's semen is a valuable commodity. The men who own the big farms and, incidentally, control the best bloodlines, are first of all businessmen, the world's richest, in fact. They sell this commodity to other breeders. And they know that mass production would cheapen the product. So, through their Jockey Club, they keep the price up by forbidding artificial insemination. Here, come take a look."

I peer through the microscope. Millions of sperm cells are thrashing about in the seminal fluid: the substance of life, each tiny organism worth a potential millions of dollars. One, perhaps, could be a future Man O'War.

"We keep a watchful eye on that product," says the vet. "It's pure gold. The moment those little sperm cells stop thrashing about it means the stallion's worn out. The Whitneys don't mine their resources to depletion. They're rich enough to wait until the stallion is rested and produces a new vein of gold. You ought to show these little sperm cells in your movie. Then you'd have the whole mystery of creation: from sperm to birth, back to mating and then to sperm all over again."

This, of course, was what I wanted to show to the Kennedys. But they weren't interested. That particular rulingclass group has other ways of producing new veins of gold.

Several weeks later, after having filmed the birth of a foal, I leave Greentree Farm to push further on in recording the life of a thoroughbred. There are weeks of shooting at the Aiken, South Carolina, winter training grounds, where the horsey ruling class watches the yearlings "broken" in the morning, plays polo in the afternoon and parties it up at night. Then up to New York to film spring and summer racing at Belmont and Saratoga.

By the beginning of 1951 I am ready to show a workprint, that is, a copy of the film in its final form, but without sound. Up to this point John Hay Whitney has seen nothing of what has been shot, although he has flown down to Aiken once to witness photography of training sequences, and has observed some of my filming at Saratoga. But of what I actually have on film, especially as regards the breeding and birth footage, he has no idea. That is to be resolved in a screening at J.H. Whitney & Co., to which he has invited the many members of his financial think tank.

"Well!" he exclaims when lights go on after the thirty-minute showing, "I've learned more about my own thorough-bred farm in this half-hour than in all these years of owning it. What do you think, gentlemen?"

"Great Stuff, Jock!" says one of the young money wizards. "I've never seen anything born before. It's a shocking and wonderful experience."

"And those breeding scenes," adds another, "I'd like my kids to see something like this. It's a terrific education."

Looking as pleased as though he's just previewed another *Gone with The Wind*, John Hay Whitney rises to shake my hand.

"Now, what about music?" he asks.

"Stock music," I reply. "You remember, I said something from Mozart. Good stuff that we'll pick up from music libraries."

"You mean canned music?"

"That's what it's called. But we'll find something that fits."

"Oh no. We have a little epic here. It must have its own original music. Get Aaron Copeland or Leonard Bernstein."

"What! Copeland? Bernstein? That'll cost me a fortune. Our contract specifies stock music."

"I'll take care of the cost. Get a first-rate composer to compose a score. We can't have a thoroughbred film downgraded with canned music even if it is Mozart's. Don't you agree, gentlemen?"

"We sure do," yes the yes-men. "You've got a little epic there."

Aaron Copeland informs me that he's up to his ears in something involving Martha Graham. Leonard Bernstein tells me he has a work in progress for the Broadway stage, besides being in the middle of his New York Philharmonic season. Virgil Thomson, although music critic for the New York *Herald Tribune* (which John Hay Whitney would eventually buy) is not interested in devoting his talents "to the glory of Mr. Whitney's silly horses." I go down the whole roster of America's leading composers, settling finally on Pulitzer Prize winner Norman Dello Joio, who is delighted to try his hand at composing a film score.

Some months later, on June 12, 1952, with commentary by Joe E. Palmer, turf writer for the *New York Herald Tribune*, and a score by Dello Joio, *Greentree Thoroughbred* is premiered at New York's Museum of Modern Art, of which naturally, considering he is John Hay Whitney, Jock Whitney is president. Next morning I awake to find myself acclaimed as maker of "one of the best documentary films in recent years," and later, the recipient of several film awards. At last I see filet mignon, not soybeans, in my future! And, to date, not a soul among the ruling class suspects that I'm a closet red.

THREE

Lifting the
Silken Curtain at the Dukes

1
Tony

The marble palace on the corner of 78th Street and Fifth Avenue, known as Duke House, was the Manhattan residence of James Buchanan Duke, "Father of the American Cigarette." Next door, in a Stanford White mansion at 972 Fifth Avenue, lived Payne Whitney (father of Jock) who, in 1927, left the then largest personal fortune ever probated. At 973 Fifth, dwelled Jock's sister, Joan Whitney Payson, who, before her death in 1974, presided over some $500,000,000, including a little philanthropy known as the New York Mets baseball team. Rounding out this modest Manhattan block at 975 Fifth, is the Louis XII chateau built by a descendant of Peter Stuyvesant, whose only philanthropy, as far as I know, is the Skid Row Bowery that eventually evolved from the huge "bouwerie" (Dutch for farm) which the Dutch inveigled from Manhattan's naive Indians for a few trinkets.

But that's far from the whole picture. Just a few blocks north lives Jackie O. herself, and a stone's throw east, descendants of Franklin Delano Roosevelt. The Upper East side of Manhattan virtually oozes with specimens of upperclass humanity known as "Beautiful People." Besides Dukes, there are Rockefellers and progeny of Rockefellers . . . Woolworths, Belmonts, Guggenheims, Phippses, Mellons, Fricks, Harknesses, Havemeyers, Carnegies, Pulitzers, Warburgs, Vanderbilts— including descendants of Mrs. Cornelius Vanderbilt, Jr., the *grande dame* who, because her ballroom could comfortably contain only those four hundred Beautiful People she considered worth knowing, gave us the term "The Four Hundred."

The list goes on and on. It is common knowledge: the Upper East side of Manhattan produces the greatest number of U.S. ambassadors, the highest amount of "charity" dollars, and, ironically, for some mysterious capitalist reason, the smallest proportionate return of personal income tax to the national treasury. A goodly amount of these charity dollars are procured by throwing some of the toniest tax-writeoff "society" parties in the nation.

"I hate 'society' parties," said Anthony ("Tony") Drexel Biddle Duke, who, for the forty-six years since he was nineteen, has thrown countless society parties. "But they are a necessary part of my life. I couldn't function without them."

But first a word about how a closet communist managed to become a confidante of the patrician Drexel Biddle Duke family. Once, during my film-making career, I shot a movie at Anthony Drexel Biddle Duke's summer place in Easthampton, New York. Many years later, noticing a news item about a forthcoming "society" party to benefit Boys Harbor, an educational institution for disadvantaged inner-city children which he heads, I said to myself: What better example of the New York ruling class than the Drexel Biddle Duke family? Tony Duke is a scion of three of the most prestigious bourgeois families in America.

In addition, he is one of the "toniest" fellows in the city. His mother, Cordelia Drexel Biddle Duke (Robertson), is a *grande dame* of Manhattan's upper class, and his brother, Angier Biddle Duke, was a U.S. Ambassador and Chief of Protocol for Presidents Kennedy and Johnson. Here I go again into the heady world of the upper-upper ruling class! I telephoned Mr. Duke, told him I was writing a book and that I'd like to look into why he and his family involve themselves in what some people might label "do-good" work for the lower classes.

"It's so nice to see you again after so long a time," he greets me at his door, a sinewy man in casual tweeds, with a prep-school military stance that makes him seem taller than his modest 5'6".

He escorts me through the office area of the Boys Harbor townhouse on East 94th Street, heading toward his private quarters. Young people, black and white, working at clerical chores, ogle me as we go by. They are the kind of street kids who were once called juvenile delinquents, a term no longer used to label problemmed youth. They have completed the Boys Harbor program for becoming viable members of society. Now they work here.

"That's the Boys Harbor idear," says Tony Duke, in a New Yorkese that, even after generations of Drexel-Biddle-Dukedom, still overlays his otherwise impeccable upperclass accent. "We take these ghetto kids, who otherwise would be totally wasted human resources, and send them back to the community as productive beings. Now they punch IBM cards instead of punching people, push pencils instead of pushing drugs."

"You said you couldn't function without society parties . . ."

"Exactly," he says, his face, with its high forehead, angular cheekbones and deep-set eyes, a beardless Abraham Lincoln's. "Boys Harbor is a voluntary agency—I hate the word charity— and we have to raise all our funds. People think because my name is Duke I sit on a mountain of money. Not so. I'm no Rockefeller who can underwrite a whole nation. We must throw parties, society parties, if you will, the kind gossip columnists love to write about."

"Society charity parties seem to be the major occupation on the Upper East Side," I suggest. "April in Paris Ball, Just One More Chance Ball, Third Street Settlement Ball, Grand Street Boys Ball . . ."

"Boys Harbor is not alone," he replies, "There are lots of people out there who need help."

I look around the room. Society party souvenirs, hunting equipment, empty coffee cups vie for space with framed pictures of Dukes and Biddles lolling in the posh watering-spots of the world. Yet even in the sloppy disorder there's an aura of upper-class self-assurance. Things are strewn about with an Old Guard *laissez faire* you'd probably not find even in so imperial an establishment as Rockefeller's Pocantico Hills. The Drexels and the Biddles, though not in the same financial league as the Rockefellers, were distinguished Mainline Philadelphia families generations before Old John D. had wiped the first scummy petroleum from his hands. I could see why parvenus would happily plunk down fat charity bucks for the chance of rubbing elbows with society at a Drexel Biddle Duke fund-raiser. And I was sure that Anthony Drexel Biddle Duke was well aware of the pulling power of his name, and dangled it as bait to fish cash out of social-climbing pockets and into his favorite charity.

"How did you ever get involved in this kind of thing, Tony?" (Everybody is on a first-name basis with Anthony Drexel Biddle Duke.) "I'd think a man with your social background would be into polo or tiger-hunting."

"I did have a shot at the playboy life, sure. But, as a teenager at St. Paul's School, I had an experience that later managed to sober me up."

"A sobering experience at St. Paul's, that training ground for upperclass playboys? What kind of sobering could possibly take place at St. Paul's except straightening out after a Sunday morning hangover? I hear that Alfred Vanderbilt spent his time there serving as bookie to his classmates."

"That's Alfred. *I* was counselor at a summer camp run by St. Paul's for post-Depression New York street kids. We became very close, I and those kids. It was a sad thing when it all had to end. But I just couldn't get the idear out of my blood."

"You've nine kids of your own, right?"

"Yes. At least it'll be nine shortly. Luly could be going off to the hospital any minute now." He glances, pleased, at a portrait of an attractive young matron who I assume is the current Mrs. Duke. "Anyway, after I left St. Paul's, I hacked together the first Boys Harbor. We built the cabins ourselves, neighbors contributed food, Mother pitched in. Fellows like John Lindsay, future Mayor of New York, Paul Moore, future Episcopal Bishop of New York, Claiborne Pell, future U.S. Senator, they all served as counselors. It limped along until World War II scattered us over the globe."

"I'll bet you made it into the Navy," I say, smiling sardonically, "John F. Kennedy, Alfred Vanderbilt, all you young men of money seem to have maneuvered yourselves into the captaincy of P.T. boats in the Pacific during the war."

"I did captain a P.T.," he replies, unresponsive to my jibe. "And it was marvelous one day to hear a voice call out from a passing boat in the middle of the Pacific, 'Hya, Mr. Duke! How's Boys Harbor?' It was a sailor who, as a kid, had gone through Boys Harbor training. I vowed then and there to start the Harbor up again when the war was over. But in a completely different way."

"How's that?"

"A summer recreation camp for blacks and Hispanics from the ghetto, many of them in great trouble, seemed too shallow. I wanted to get deep down inside. To provide therapy and tutorial programs, teach remedial reading, mechanical skills, performing arts. In other words, to provide the education these kids were not getting. As a result, a boy like Albie Williams, a black kid who didn't even own a pair of shoes when he came to us, is now a Ph.D. and professor of literature. Leroy Saunders, once a so-called juvenile delinquent, is an outstanding New York City cop. Nathan Allen is a black high up in the Justice Department."

There is pride in Anthony Drexel Biddle Duke's eye as he announces these successes, not unlike that of a corporation president reporting to his stockholders a good bottom line. Yet I cannot help but wonder whether this affable bearer of three great family names, this urbane product of St. Paul's and Princeton University, is simply carrying on the ancient *noblesse oblige* tradition of "caring for the poor." That is, whether he would be doing this sort of thing were he not a Drexel Biddle Duke from the marble mansions of the Upper East Side. Why, for instance, instead of working to see that shoeless Albie Williams becomes a Ph.D., does he not work to see that a society which makes hereditary Drexel Biddle Dukes multi-millionaires and in which millions of shoeless Albie Williams never become Ph.D.s, is changed at the core? For what, after all, does it mean if, in a population of millions condemned to poverty, a token Albie Williams or two becomes a Ph.D.? These questions, however, a closet communist keeps to himself, else the interview would surely be over.

"I feel that there should be Boys Harbors all over the nation," says Tony Duke, as if in answer to my reflections. "There's a terrible danger that if these kids are exposed to improper influences they can become prey to incorrect idears. What's going on in East Africa right now, for instance, can lead to a blood bath. It can also have an echo effect on our minority populations that would be devastating. I can foresee big racial trouble in this country. All that anger and suspicion, if fed by hostile people, can easily turn into communism. If Boys Harbor has one major project today, it's this: to open up minds to the proper influences."

Oh? Is fear of communism, then, the real reason for Boys Harbor and all those other "charities" for the disadvantaged? And what "proper influences?" Those of the ruling classes, who wish to maintain a secure position at the top of the heap?

The phone interrupts and Tony Duke picks it up to converse with Luly, who, I gather, still has not come across with that ninth individual needed to complete the Drexel Biddle Duke baseball team. Up to now all my contact with members of the

41

Social Register world has been of a business nature, such as providing them with movies, photographs and other indulgences. But here, for the first time, I am third party to a personal conversation of a most intimate nature. I now have Tony Duke winking at me and discussing his "Mom" with his wife. (Does one, in the presence of an outsider, usually refer to a mother who entertains the Duchess of Windsor as "Mom," or am I being "adopted," as others useful to his cause are admitted to his private world?) I also hear him ask Luly whether she had noticed Brother "Angie" (U.S. Ambassador and Chief of Protocol Angier Biddle Duke) picking his nose, as usual, in the background of the TV broadcast President Carter has just made. Whatever the purpose of this disarming informality in my presence, if indeed there is a purpose, I suddenly get a feeling of having been made privy to intimacies at Buckingham Palace.

"Luly is remarkable. You must come to lunch and meet her," says Tony Duke, returning to our dialogue. "She's a refugee from Castro. But she's adapted a hundred percent to the Boys Harbor idear. All my other marriages were a little shattered by the Harbor."

"How do you mean?"

"Well, Alice couldn't take it, Betty got fed up, and Didi finally threw up her hands. I guess they all felt that our lives were invaded by too many of the Harbor kids coming up to the main house and jumping in and out of the pool."

"I remember. That summer I shot the film at Easthampton. Seeing all those black ghetto hands pawing your little white Cordelia, I couldn't quite understand it. Coming from her social background, I thought, the then-Mrs. Duke would be appalled."

"I can understand Betty's feelings," says Tony Duke wistfully. "The Harbor took a lot of my time and some ladies don't appreciate that."

He rises and takes a book from a shelf. I recognize it: *The Dukes of Durham*, which I've previously skimmed. Even the little I've read is fascinating, for, despite its having been published by the family-endowed Duke University, a story has nevertheless seeped through of the two "robber baron" Duke brothers who clawed their way up from the boondocks to leave manor houses, charities and dogooder descendants in the marble mansions of the Upper East Side of Manhattan. Benjamin Buchanan Duke, Tony's grandfather, was one of the two Dukes who, in the last century, cornered the tobacco market and, under the famous "Bull Durham" slogan, soon had a $500-million monopoly and each a Duke mansion on Fifth Avenue.

"This book tells what a son-of-a-bitch James Duke, my granduncle was, and what a sweet guy my grandfather Ben was, but also very shrewd," says Tony, as he flips through *The Dukes of Durham*. "Teddy Roosevelt tried to trust-bust them, but they gave him the slip. Dumped all their tobacco holdings and went into textiles and Duke Power. My father, Angier Buchanan Duke, a typical rich playboy of the era, married my mother, Cordelia Drexel Biddle, a Philadelphia Mainliner, when she was only seventeen."

Ah yes, Duke Power and Philadelphia Biddles! Isn't there a documentary film called *Harlan County, USA* (made by people like myself) which shows how Duke Power murdered coalminers in union-busting tactics in Kentucky? And Philadelphia Biddles—not one but *two* of *nouveau riche* Ben Duke's children made marriages to Philadelphia Mainline Biddles. Besides Angier Buchanan Duke marrying Cordelia Drexel Biddle, his sister, Mary Duke, married Cordelia's brother Anthony, a double shot at climbing the social ladder. Is Tony Duke, then, merely making amends for his robber baron inheritance? Or is his Boys Harbor "idear" a genuine expression of love for his fellowman?

"My father died when I was six," he says. "My stepfather, T. Markoe Robertson, although a great guy, had little time for us. So both my brother Angie and I were raised by Grandfather Biddle."

"The guy who kept alligators in his living room? Didn't they do a Hollywood movie about him called *The Happiest Millionaire*?"

"Yes. He was a Marine Colonel, judo enthusiast, bayonet fighter and gentleman boxing champ. President Teddy Roosevelt and evangelist Billy Sunday were his heroes. He even conducted his own Bible classes for the disadvantaged. He loved Boys Harbor, truly did. Came down to the summer camp in the early days, taught us to box and preached to us."

And even offered to put together for Woodrow Wilson a full division of his disadvantaged Bible Classers as cannon fodder for the 1914 War to Save Capitalist Democracy. Perpetuating the System which had made him the happiest millionaire was, I felt certain, the motive, however unconscious, behind all that Bible-waving to the disadvantaged by the "eccentric" Marine Colonel who admired the Jingo Teddy Roosevelt and his imperialist charge up Cuba's San Juan Hill. But was the same true for his grandson and his Boys Harbor idear?

"You must visit Mother," suggests Tony. "It's wonderful to see people of different means—black ghetto kids who made it to our board of directors, white corporation presidents, Duke and Biddle family members—all dancing happily together at our Boys Harbor parties. And Mother is the magnet that draws them there."

2
Mother

"Mother" lives on Park Avenue, the Park Avenue of the old established rich. Mother's apartment is in a quietly fashionable building designed by T. Markoe Robertson, her now-deceased second husband. Its drawing room is faced with mahogany panels shipped to Manhattan from the ancestral Biddle mansion in Mainline Philadelphia.

As I arrive a uniformed doorman helps me out of the taxi and, consulting a memo from on high—presumably from Mother's social secretary—approves my ascent to her quarters. I have never entered a place as discreetly elegant as this before, except as a tradesman admitted through the back door. Now I'm coming, as a closet red, to "have a Dubonnet" with the octogenarian Biddle Duke *doyenne*, even as princes and duchesses and superstars have so often done. To be sure, I am still something of a tradesman (a writer plying his trade) but Tony Duke has arranged the visit on so personal a level—"Don't let Mother get you high on Dubonnet," he had warned me—that in the elevator I am already a little high. A writer/observer does not, after all, get to chat every day with a lady whose forebears were officers in Washington's army and go back, not to 1776, but to 1676. Moreover, after the interview there is to be one of those intimate little fund-raising parties at which, Tony said, I would meet some "nice people."

The walls of the drawing room, where I await Cordelia Drexel Biddle Duke Robertson, are so heavily hung with photographs of "Beautiful People" who have passed through her eighty-some years that I can just about find an exposed section of that fine old Mainline Philadelphia mahogany panel. The grand piano also holds a gallery of Beautiful Ones, arranged around an autographed portrait of the Duchess of Windsor. In a framed snapshot I see Mother, with her young sons, Angier and Anthony, and her brother, Ambassador Anthony Drexel Biddle, Jr. They are chumming it up with exiled ex-King Alfonso of Spain at his hunting lodge in Austria. Another feudal expatriate's picture, Prince Serge Obolensky of Czarist Russia, vies for space on the Steinway with a snapshot of Grandfather Biddle, the Bible-toting gentleman boxing champ, who is kicking the bejesus out of somebody in a judo match.

Fish—tiny, sculptured silver fish—in enormous collections, lie in silver trays in every corner of the room, like sardines in huge open cans. Snuff boxes and antique gold watches by the dozens, in addition to bisque, porcelain and Dresden figurines, gleam from every mantel. Cordelia Drexel Biddle Duke Robertson is obviously a collector of expensive things as well as expensive people. She also has great trust in humanity (either that or she never entertains larcenous guests) for as my eye sweeps over the miniature treasures I think: How easily one could filch a pocketful and walk out undetected.

A tiny barking dachshund interrupts my visual tour, and growls ominously as though it detects my larcenous thoughts.

"Peaches! Stop it now!" says Cordelia Drexel Biddle Duke Robertson as she strides toward me extending her hand. (The gesture disarms me somewhat: I am not sure if I am expected to kiss the hand, but, having rehearsed for such a possibility, I peck it just above the knuckles.) "It's so nice to see you," she drawls in a gravelly Mainline voice that brings to mind Tallulah Bankhead.

"I'm charmed to meet you, Mrs. Robertson," I respond, as though I'm an alumnus of Harrow instead of the Workers School for Marxist Studies.

"You're writing a book, Tony tells me . . ."

"Yes, about the great institutions of New York, of which you are one."

"My sons—*they're* the institutions. I'm so proud of them. Will you have something to drink?"

"Dubonnet."

"Ah yes, *goooood* boy. Try my mix of red and white."

Cordelia Drexel Biddle Duke Robertson is wearing, as Enid Emy, The *New York Times* society reporter, might note, plain black pumps and a black woolen frock, unadorned except with a simple brooch and necklace which, to my inexpert eye, seems the most unpretentious of costume jewelry. There are neither diamonds nor emeralds on her fingers. She is a model of patrician good taste for an afternoon chit-chat. As we sit down, Peaches, having put me in place with upperclass canine growls, leaps onto the sofa and finds a comfortable spot in her lady's lap.

"That Boys Harbor! Most *Wonnnnderful*," says Cordelia Drexel Biddle Duke Robertson, stretching out the word in a hoarse musical basso. "Tony has this great love for those poor children. He'd bring them down to our little place at Southampton and talk to them. You see, he's full of religion, Tony, full of humility. Got it from my father."

"Tony said his grandfather, Colonel Biddle, made a man of him. Taught him boxing."

"Taught *me* boxing! Skinny little thing that I was, I had a *fieeeeerce* rabbit punch."

"You?"

"Yes indeed. We had a boxing ring in back of the house, so all of us children had to box. Father was the best gentleman boxer in the country. Sparred with all the professional champions. Taught us to fence, taught us religion, everything. With both boxing and religion I could take on stevedores as well as bishops. I loved him with a passion."

"As a girl, Joan Whitney went to all the professional fights with her father. Did you do that too?"

"Didn't have to. The fighters came to us. We had more exhibition matches in our backyard boxing ring than Madison Square Garden. Father would beat them all up. Then he'd have them in for dinner."

She fingered two ringlets of hair on her forehead, which was framed by long dark tresses, like a teenage girl's.

"Father had a heart of gold. If anybody made him mad, he'd belt him one and see he got fired. Then he'd cry. Weep real tears. And if he had you fired—you'd always *haaave* to lose your job, he'd see to that—then he'd repent and get you a better job."

"He'd see that you lost your job?"

"Oh, you just *haaad* to lose your job . . . get him mad and he'd see you were fired. But then, wherever you were, he'd find you and get you a still better job."

"In what business? His own?"

"Noaaaah! Father had no *bus*iness. What would he do with a *bus*iness? No, he wasn't like that. He just loved people. First of all he was very religious. Had these *huuuuuuge* Bible classes, the Anthony J. Drexel Biddle Bible Classes, all over the place. He believed everything in the Bible."

"Literally?"

"Absolutely."

"But there are admittedly at least 1,000 total contradictions in the Bible."

"Of *courrrrse*! But you dare mention that and he'd beat you up."

She lets out a raucous Tallulah Bankhead laugh that sends Peaches into a barking frenzy. At this point lunch is wheeled in by a servant—platters of colorful dips and raw vegetables arranged in those painfully unappetizing compositions one sees in the pages of *McCalls*.

"Have a bite," she says, feeding a cucumber slice to Peaches.

"Just a little dip," I reply.

"Have a *biiiig* dip," she sings, "and another Dubonnet."

A big dip. That, frankly, is precisely what I'm fantasizing at the moment. A big dip into the glamorous world presided over by this lady. Park Avenue, Southampton, lunch in her "little" place with Cee Zee and Jackie O. Cocktails with Truman C. and Andy W. Skiing the white slopes of Switzerland, sailing the blue waters off Cannes, box at the opera, April in Paris Ball . . . here it all is, open sesame, for the asking, if you would but be a clever sycophant. I am this very day sipping Dubonnet at the fountainhead: Cordelia Drexel Biddle Duke Robertson, a lady who is the very model of a swinging rulingclass duchess—with lunch at Tony and Luly's to follow, and an invite to a Duke "society" ball to top it off. In this court of the top strata of the ruling class, I discover not brackish water but rare champagne, and I now understand Scott Fitzgerald's fascination with the super-rich. Beware, closet communist, lest fantasy entice you out of the closet to become an adoring capitalist!

"Tony loved those poor little fellows, mostly colored," Cordelia Drexel Biddle Duke Robertson resumes. "He'd find them under the stove somewhere, the mother sleeping with strange men, that sort of thing. He'd pick out the most pathetic, feed them, teach them: prayer, exercise, everything. He made *mennnn* of them."

"But wasn't Tony a playboy?" I ask, hoping to get another view.

"He *is* a playboy," she whistles, taking a chesty drag on a cigarette. "Four marriages, lots of girl friends—Diana Barrymore, in particular. Now all those boys he taught are gone. Jobs, marriage, children. They come for dinner sometimes. They're *greaaaaaat* gentlemen. But at the moment Tony is more married than ever. He's so in love with Luly—madly. But I've always thought he was madly in love with everybody, so there you are."

"And what about Angier, your eldest son?"

"Angie? I call him Bunny. He's had lots of affairs, too. Poor Maria-Luisa, his wife. I loved her with all my heart. She was coming home to Southampton after helping Bunny see off the King of Saudi Arabia. This tiny plane—the door opened and she was swept out. So busted up they wouldn't let Bunny see her. He almost went insane. Kept knocking his head against the wall and crying, 'I want to kiss her hand! I want to kiss her hand!' Ah, she was so beautiful. A Spanish marquesa who looked like the Duchess of Alba."

The Dubonnet has put a youthful glow on Cordelia Biddle Duke's octogenarian face, and the voice is more Tallulah now— throaty and trilled like the sound of a bassoon. It is Speaker of the House Bankhead's witty and uninhibited daughter who is sitting beside me on the sofa, sweeping with aristocratic gesture the long dark hair from her face.

"That gesture—sweeping your hair," I say, "it reminds me of Tallulah Bankhead. Did you know Tallulah, Mrs. Robertson?"

"Of *cawzzze*, dahling," she replies, mimicking the lady. "Very well. Many, many parties."

"You're a double for her, not only in looks but in sound and movement. Did you know that?"

"Oh yes. Taxi men, they always look twice and ask, 'Are you what's-her-name?' And I always tell them, 'Now if you know your newspapers, you'd know she's dead.' And they look so annoyed because they think I'm just fooling. But the younger ones seem disappointed because they remember Tallulah's reputation."

"How do you mean?"

"Really? You can't guess? Once she said to me, 'Cordelia, there's nothing I haven't done, no sensation I haven't had.' Oh she was a scream, a naughty, naughty girl. I can't imagine her married."

My little chat with Cordelia Drexel Biddle Duke Robertson has, at least for the moment, come to an end. Guests are scheduled to arrive shortly for a late afternoon cocktail party. Servants begin arranging buffets, barmen lay out glasses and snacks, flowers are placed around. I gather up my notes and things while Cordelia retires to freshen up.

"Sex goddess! Heiress! Cover girl!" exclaims the first arrival, a young man who falls into the arms of the now-revitalized octogenarian hostess. He is accompanied by a friend who wears a Moslem-type skull cap and a champagne-colored beard.

"Meet Liv," says Cordelia, introducing me. "Same name as my brother, Livingston Biddle. And this, Liv, is Stanley . . ."

"Stanley? You're pulling my leg, Cordelia. You're pulling the old Livingston/Stanley bit."

"No, no! Stanley . . . *reeeeally*. He brings me this *diviiiiine* jewelry. When I want something he comes to me."

"And I'm Tambourines," announces the friend with the Moslem cap. "I play tambourines with the Richie Family combo."

Stanley opens a case and lays out a sampling of scintillating rings, pins, necklaces and brooches.

"Are those real?" I ask.

"Of course they're real," says Stanley. "Real *costume*. They're my own creations."

"Nobody wears Cartier anymore," says Cordelia. "The little man from Cartier who brings jewelry on a velvet tray is a thing of the past."

"Looks like Kenny Lane's things," I say.

"It's *aaaall* Kenny Lane," replies Cordelia. "Elegant costume jewelry. Kenny is the one who made the little man from Cartier passe. Stan had a fuss with Kenny, as, of course, everybody eventually does. Left him to set up his own shop." She picks up three brooches, fingers them carefully. "I think these are such fun. What do you think?"

"Cordelia," interrupts Tambourines, "do you have anybody in your family out in Indiana working in a bank? Because I read in the paper that somebody by the name of Biddle embezzled over a half a million dollars from Indiana National Bank."

"Oh sure," says Cordelia. "Got to be one of my family," and we all guffaw. "Aren't these divine!" she picks up another brace of gleaming knick-knacks. "I think I hear voices" she says. "Tonykins that you?"

Tony Duke walks into the drawing room accompanied by a group of guests. He wears gray flannel slacks, white shirt with a striped rep tie and navy blue blazer adorned with the patch of St. Paul's School. He looks every bit the blueblood dropping into his club for a late afternoon nip, while his companions, a motley group—mostly women fresh with frizzed hair from the beauty parlor—are obviously nouveau-riche middleclass with some time and money on their hands. I can tell from their self-conscious smiles, as they drink up the atmosphere, that many of them are elbow-rubbers from Boys Harbor's mailing list who have been permitted to sniff about Cordelia Duke's home.

"Mother!" exclaims Tony. "Have a nice afternoon?"

"*Ooooooohh* yes. Liv is *suuuuuuch* a darling."

"You see, didn't I tell you?" Tony says to me. "And Luly

is so looking forward to meeting you too."

More guests are now arriving and soon the room is filled with an uncomfortable mix of authentic Beautiful People and People-From-The-Other-Side-Of-The-New-York-Central-Railroad-Tracks. Tony Duke now calls for everybody's attention. We all face forward to listen.

"Briefly I want to remind you of the great party coming up at the St. Regis Hotel which you've already heard so much about. But first I want to welcome all of you to my mother's house—where is she?—Oh, yes, she's over there. Mother is uh— an amazing lady . . ."

"Aaah*maaaaaay*zing!" Cordelia echoes in her Tallulah number, now ripened by Dubonnet and excitement. The room responds with a rollicking wave of laughter, as though Elizabeth II had shouted "Horseshit!" at a Windsor Palace soiree.

". . . Mother's one of the tougher, more agile members of the Boys Harbor board, and whenever things start to lag at a meeting she says, 'Get on with it! Say what you're going to say and get it over with.' And so, before Mother starts shouting, we'd better get on with the business. We'll be sharing the spotlight together at the St. Regis party, we, you and all the celebrities. As far as our board is concerned we're hitting hard on the issues of today. That's the Boys Harbor idear: rescuing young people who, when abandoned, learn to steal, push, mug, murder, and die. Parties like the one we're asking you to support are tremendously important. That's where our dollars come from . . ."

3
El Duke

Now for "Bunny."

Who could be a better example of the old established ruling class of Manhattan than Angier Biddle Duke, the world's most urbane diplomat. "Angie," as his friends call him, or Bunny, as his mother dubbed him, lives in River House, the East Side's snootiest apartment complex. So snooty, in fact, that Gloria Vanderbilt was denied a residence because she knew too many black people.

Angie was born in the Benjamin Duke House, one of Fifth Avenue's oldest remaining mansions. At 36, he had been the youngest ambassador in U.S. history, and, as chief of Protocol for both Presidents Kennedy and Johnson, had personally met more monarchs and chiefs of state than perhaps any man in the world.

Both JFK and LBJ well knew what they were doing when they selected Angier Biddle Duke for the job of welcoming foreign dignitaries to the United States. No one was better equipped to impress leaders of newly independent Third World nations who flooded into Washington during those two administrations.

Even his name—Biddle Duke, like those of hyphenated British upperclass dynasties—had just the right tone of snootiness for a U.S. Chief of Protocol. In addition, Drexel Biddle Dukes had long been accustomed, over the generations, to having U.S. Presidents, foreign nobility, even kings, as intimate companions; Angie himself, as a boy, had chased rabbits at Bourbon King Alfonso's hunting lodge in Austria.

Too, his equally formidable entertaining prowess. He and his then-wife, the former Luisa de Arana, granddaughter of the Spanish Marques de Campo Real, a man who lived in a house built by ancestors 1200 years ago, were world-famous for the quality of their parties. This was a fact which nouveau-riche Massachusetts Senator, John F. Kennedy, no doubt made note of for future use on occasional visits to the Duke estate at Southampton.

Finally, his looks: tall, slim, suave. No one in the entire world, except perhaps the Duke of Edinburgh, in real life, or David Niven, in film, looked as well in striped trousers and double-breasted jacket as did Angier Biddle Duke.

Thus it was that the plebeian Catholic President selected as his official host America's most aristocratic WASP, a choice to which JFK's Yahoo Texas successor—even more in need of social polish—also acceded. And, on becoming Mayor of New York, Abraham D. Beame, another chap in need of social polish, prevailed upon Angier Biddle Duke, an unemployed Democrat during the Nixon administration, to become his dollar-a-year Commissioner of Civic Affairs and Public Events. In this job he would perform for Gracie Mansion many of the same functions he had managed for the White House.

The idea of sitting down with so formidable a member of the ruling class in the intimacy of his home was for me, an abscure closet communist, something on the order of having a private drink with the President in his White House quarters.

And even though I was going to Angier Biddle Duke's by arrangement with his brother Tony, I was anything but at ease as I entered River House lobby.

"I'm Angier Duke. How are you?" says the tall, balding man with the aquiline nose when I get off the elevator that opens directly into his apartment. "Let me take your coat."

No servants in this grand establishment? Or is this Professional Greeter so accustomed to welcoming people that he sometimes forgets who is the Prince and who the Pauper?

"Fine," I say, handing him a Hardy Amies greatcoat I've borrowed for the occasion from a fashionable friend. (He himself is dressed in the plainest of casuals.) "It's a great pleasure to meet you, Sir Duke, uh . . . I mean Mr. Duke."

We both laugh, I in embarrassment, he to put me at ease.

"It's a common occurrence," he says. "President Eisenhower, having heard the nickname Angie, once addressed me as Mr. Angel. And when I was ambassador to Spain, some people thought Duke was a title. They called me El Duke."

He leads me into the library, a beautifully-appointed, daylight-flooded room, the brilliant decorator colors of which are darkened only by the hundreds of leather-bound volumes that line the shelves.

"Would you like some oatmeal—breakfast of some kind?" he asks. "I've just finished with the Exercycle and haven't had my coffee yet."

"Love some."

"I'll have to make it for you myself," he apologizes. "The servants are all off—some sort of holiday. My wife and son are skiing in Switzerland. Everybody's away. Won't take a minute."

In his absence I walk around the room, amused by the idea that the man whose job had been to see that people like Charles de Gaulle got truffles and Khrushchev borscht at White House dinners, is, with his own hands cooking up a pot of porridge for me. And the idea of plebian porridge counterpoints well with the regal settees and divans which, through a doorway, I see scattered around the drawing room, presumably by some such august overseer of upperclass style as Billy Baldwin. Even the English Regency library, with its lush carpets, silver trophies and framed mementoes from the world's most Beautiful and Significant People, radiates chic. The books on the shelves, I notice, are in large part the most ordinary of popular works. But they are bound in extraordinarily exquisite leather. The Ambassador, it seems, has all his reading material custom-clothed—even his speeches and newspaper clippings. His literature is every bit as dapper as himself.

"Now what is it you're after?" he asks, as he places a serving of steaming oatmeal in front of me and sits down to one himself. "Tony tells me you're writing about Manhattan. How do I fit into that? I should think I was more Washington or international than Manhattan."

"Yes, you undoubtedly are global. But you're also Manhattan. You and Tony were born and raised on the Upper East Side, and you live here now. The Drexel Biddle Dukes are a landmark of the area."

"But I'm in a kind of hiatus now."

"Makes no difference. You are the man who, as Commissioner of Civic Affairs and Public Events, presents the face of New York City to itself and to the world. What I want to know is what's involved in that function and what kind of person it is who performs it."

"Okay. That gives us something of a direction" he agrees, stroking his large Adam's apple. "Both U.S. Chief of Protocol and New York City Commissioner of Public Events have one objective in common: to present the respective Chief Executive in the best possible light. So, before I get into the City aspect, let me give a couple of examples of the problems involved on the national level. You'll see how the same thing pops up in the City."

He pours a second draft of coffee into my cup, gets up and paces about the room.

"In the first year of John Kennedy's presidency thirty-three new states exploded into independence. And all of them wanted a meeting with the U.S. President, because that's one of the main ways of legitimizing their sovereignty. Now this was absurd. Here was Europe dying on the vine: NATO, Common Market, all the pressures of the East-West struggle. The President just couldn't neglect our traditional European allies and instead receive one of those new leaders that first year." As Angier Biddle Duke talks he keeps realigning books that have fallen askew on the shelves.

"Well, we couldn't bring Willy Brandt over: that would make de Gaulle unhappy. We couldn't invite de Gaulle: that would give him pre-eminence in Europe. So State suggested inviting the Grand Duchess of Luxembourg in honor of the 40th anniversary of her accession to the throne—longest ruling monarch in Europe. A few days later I happened to be in Kenny O'Donnell's office, and the President stuck his head out the door.

" 'Come in here!' he barked. 'Did you get a load of this memo from State?'

" 'Yes, sir, I did.'

" 'You agree with it?'

" 'Yes, sir, I do.'

" 'Of all the things . . . I mean, that's what's wrong with the Gawddamn State Department. I've never heard of a nuttier thing in all my life. Here we are in this East/West confrontation with all its problems, and they ask me to receive the Grand Duchess of Luxembourg. Don't you think that's complete insanity?'

" 'No, sir, I don't'

" 'Well, listen, there's no time to talk. Go in the next room and dictate a less than one-page memo on why you don't think this is sheer stupidity.' "

Angier Biddle Duke, as he explains it, did not use the State Department rationale of "the longest ruling monarch in Europe." Instead, in his memo, he pointed out that Adolph Hitler had forced the Grand Duchess of Luxembourg to become a refugee, a fact which had so moved President Roosevelt that he sent a destroyer for her, making her the first refugee to be put up at the White House.

"I told the President that it would be very strange indeed if, at this particular hour in European history, a U.S. President should turn his back on a ruler who was a symbol of triumph over tyranny. Well, he bought it and the Duchess came. But he couldn't resist taking a dig at me. 'You see what you got me into,' he growled just before going into the big luncheon we gave for her. 'You and your *Graaaahnd* Duchess. Here goes two hours of my day." '

The telephone breaks into our joint laughter and Angier Biddle Duke picks it up.

"Governor who? Oh, Governor Curtis, right. The Mayor and I are trying to work it out. Yes, I'll be over on the Hill at four Tuesday. Right, fine. See you then."

He replaces the phone with the boredom of a man who might as easily expect a call from outer space as from the luminaries of this world. "Now where were we? Oh yes, Protocol. You not only have to *up*grade VIP's, sometimes your job is to gracefully *down*grade them. Can you imagine having to downgrade the Chief Justice of the United States?"

"I can't think of anyone who could do it with more aplomb than you, Mr . . ."

"You may call me Angie . . . we're not in the Oval Office now," he says pleasantly. "Downgrading Earl Warren! That's the first job I had from President Kennedy as Chief of Protocol. Congress had just passed a new law providing that the Speaker of the House, instead of the Chief Justice, would succeed to the Presidency if both the President and Vice-President became incapacitated. But the order of official precedence remained the same."

"Official precedence?"

"How they rank at official functions. That remained President, Vice-President, Chief Justice, and then Speaker of the House. So the President sent me over to tell Earl Warren that he was going to change the official order and make it conform to the new law of the land."

He notices an unfastened shirt-button violating protocol and pauses to correct it.

"Anyway, I went over to the Supreme Court. And I can tell you it's a very impressive piece of business going into the Chief Justice's office—like going to the White House for the first time. It was not an easy thing to do, as you can imagine: telling Earl Warren that he was going to be downgraded.

" 'Well,' the Chief Justice growled, 'this is a fine time to do this. We're trying to enforce the civil rights laws in Mississippi and Alabama, trying to upgrade the Supreme Court. And here the President is downgrading it in the eyes of the American people. Will you kindly tell him that?'

" 'Yes, sir, I will. But I'm here to tell you what's happening and what's going to be done.'

" 'He should choose a better time to do it.'

"I went back to the President with the message and he said he got the Chief Justice's point. 'But what we'll do,' he explained, 'is we won't announce it. Just let it happen. If the press picks it up, fine. But there'll be no making it obvious that I'm downgrading the Supreme Court, which is not my intention at all.' This is a story I've never told before," Angier Biddle Duke informs me. "Perhaps I shouldn't have told it to you. But I'm going to talk about it for the first time in a speech to the new Cabinet wives in Washington next week. So I guess it's all right."

Once more the phone. This time Duke University, something about the Duke family archives (certain rulingclass families have their very own universities: Rockefeller University, Vanderbilt University, Duke University). And these centers of learning gratefully perform odd jobs for those families, such as, in the Duke instance, preserving for the edification of posterity notable historical events like Angier Biddle Duke telling new Cabinet wives how to behave in Washington.

"I'll give you one more example of what's involved in protocol work before we move to the city scene," he resumes. "The Kennedy visit to de Gaulle, for instance. I went to Paris six weeks in advance. We planned every second of the President's time. It was a tough bargaining session, trading off what our host thought important against what we thought important, which is one of the main functions of protocol work."

"Mrs. Kennedy went along with her husband, as I remember."

"Yes, and the incredible reception she received caused the President playfully to refer to himself as the man who accompanied Jacqueline Kennedy to France. They put them up at the Quai D'Orsay. Next day de Gaulle arrived for the ride up the Champs Elysees. But there was one helluva rainfall which nobody had exactly bargained for. The President looked out the door and saw de Gaulle all resplendent in his magnificent uniform.

" 'We'll put up the rooftop on the car against the rain,' de Gaulle said."

"I'll bet JFK didn't go for that," I volunteer. "I never saw him wear a coat. I mean, he always seemed determined to project a youthful image."

"Perhaps. But he did say, 'Oh no, Mr. President, we can't put up the rooftop.'

" 'Fine,' said de Gaulle. 'Get your coat and we'll go.'

" 'No, no, I won't put on a raincoat,' said JFK, setting off a battle of wills.

" 'You won't put on a raincoat?' said de Gaulle, growing irritated.

" 'No, sir, I don't think I need one.'

"So de Gaulle promptly took off his own coat and handed it to an aide. And the two of them rode up the Champs Elysees in the open Citroen, with rain pouring down in buckets."

"And probably hating each other . . ." I add.

"I won't say what was in their minds," replies the former Chief of Protocol, diplomatically. "But, as you see, there are always unknown variables to the script you plan. That's what makes the work so fascinating."

Another telephone call. Now it's the headmaster of St. Paul's, the prep school that turns out the likes of Angier Biddle Duke to fit them for the role of palliating the bad manners of America's Presidents.

"I guess I can't downgrade *him*, can I?" says Angie, covering the phone's mouthpiece with his hand. "Will you bear with me while I see what his problem is?" And he goes on to ward off a proposed visit from the moulder of rulingclass gentlemen in a manner much more ingratiating than JFK's handling the raincoat incident, while at the same time making the headmaster feel he's one of the most important persons on earth.

Now we come to somebody that patricians such as Angier Biddle Duke actually consider one of the most important persons on earth. Her Britainnic Majesty was the centerpiece of the biggest protocol production in his entire career. *Star*: Queen of England. *Cast*: millions. *Setting*: world's most colossal city. *Time*: Bicentennial year of the richest nation in history. In July, 1976, Elizabeth II would, on a state visit to the United States, spend a day in New York City. It would be the apex of the year, coming as it did between the Fourth of July with its Tall Ships Festival, and the opening of the Democratic Presidential Convention at Madison Square Garden. During those days the city would reach a state of euphoria it had seldom experienced. And Angier Biddle Duke, now New York City's Commissioner of Civic Affairs and Public Events, was the central person making all decisions on every step connected with, not only the Tall Ships and the Democratic Convention but also, and most especially, the Royal Visit. The official good manners of the City of New York, now host to the monarch of the mother country from which the nation had wrested independence, was in his hands.

This is not a matter that one resolves by taking tips from Emily Post's *Handbook of Etiquette*. Arranging an official visit to New York City of a head of state, and, particularly, the Queen of England, is a project of enormous delicacy.

Much intricate sparring takes place. Representatives of both host and guest try to slant the trip for maximum political mileage for their principals. Powerful pressure groups, anxious to exploit the visit for their own interests, are also problems, as is, of course, the question of security. But almost as critical are the personal characteristics of both guest and host, and the details of how to blend them into fruitful unity. Additionally, there are considerations of good taste and of sensibilities. In matters such as these who else but Angier Biddle Duke?

"We worked an entire year just for the Queen's one-day visit. Meetings with the British Ambassador, the Queen's private secretary, Scotland Yard, Secret Service, members of the British colony in New York. A game of chess, with moves and checkmates by both planning parties. For instance, New York's Mayor never goes to the airport to meet a visiting head of state. Once you establish that precedent you become a prisoner of it, and if you make an exception you downgrade somebody. But everyone thought: 'Gee! The Queen of England, the country that we once rebelled against, coming to us in our Bicentennial year, and we can't even make an exception for her?' No, sir, we didn't. But we cooked up something much more dramatic."

This involved having the Queen land at Newark airport, where the Governor of New Jersey would accompany her in a motorcade to a pier at Bayonne. The royal yacht, *Brittania*, would be waiting there, and, with the Queen aboard, would steam up New York Bay to the Battery. This would be a spectacular event, and, moreover, would seem uncontrived.

"But the high point," said Angie, with obvious pride, "was the Queen of England standing at the feet of George Washington—that magnificent statue at the Sub-Treasury Building in Wall Street where he took his oath of office. And it worked out fine. We had to make some compromises, of course: those pressures I mentioned. Trinity Church wanted that business of the Queen receiving the symbolic rent of peppercorn from the Pastor (the Windsors still receive *actual* rent from American properties) and the British wanted what they call a 'walkabout,' that is, having the Queen go out among the people—something our security dislikes. But is was not too far from the Sub-Treasury to the church, so we yielded.

"When the day came, the people went wild. They broke the barriers, the Secret Service lost control. It was a good-natured crowd, but they pushed and shoved and tried to touch her, and she got seriously separated from the Duke of Edinburgh by about forty feet. Now, the Secret Service doesn't like having to lay on with fists, but there is always the threat of the IRA, some Oswald or James Earl Ray, and for about thirty seconds we were, shall I say, shaking in our boots."

"How did the Queen hold up under the stress?"

"With her usual aplomb. Then there was that astounding ride up Third Avenue to the Waldorf-Astoria Hotel. They did something curious which is not usual in New York. Both the Queen and the Duke stood up through the sunroof of the car—a practice they are used to at home—and rode that way clear up to the hotel. This in itself created a sensation. It was the pinnacle of the Bicentennial Year, and one of the highlights of my career. The Queen's private secretary was knighted for his work on the project."

"And you? What was your reward?"

"My reward was in the work itself. And it was even more gratifying because, as things are now, nothing is more important than rescuing England. She's in terrible trouble. Our Atlantic Alliance, all of the Western world and its values are at stake on the fate of England. Anything that helps rescue her is worth doing, and that visit, I think, helped rebuild her prestige."

"You Drexel Biddle Dukes all seem to be rescuers," I observe.

"How do you mean?"

"Well, Tony rescues blacks from the ghetto. Your grandfather, the old Marine Colonel, rescues sinners with his Drexel Biddle Bible Classes, and you once headed the International Rescue Committee, the organization that whisks refugees out of certain countries. I remember reading about your going to Hungary to rescue victims of the 1956 uprising." (U.S.—supported 1956 counter-revolution is, of course, what I wanted to say.)

"Yes, the Rescue Committee had its people there, and I

went three days later. We brought many refugees to this country. That's the charm and fascination of the work. You see, it's not only the humanitarian issue, it's also political. There's a battle going on between democracy and dictatorship, between our values and theirs, and those refugees are visible symbols of the failure of their society. So it's important we give them a helping hand. Both Tony and I went to South Viet Nam too, many times, he to help with displaced youth, I with political refugees."

I wonder, as I listen to this impassioned member of America's elite of elites, why there was no such deep concern for victims of the dictatorship which strangled democratic Chile? How is it that his International Rescue Committee, which is reported to be but another clandestine arm of the CIA war against socialist countries, never rescued victims of the despotic Shah of Iran, or victims of the Indonesian dictatorship that massacred thousands of Communists and currently holds thousands more in dungeons? Is it really, as he suggests, "a struggle between democracy and dictatorship," or rather between capitalism and socialism? After all, Tony Duke himself told me that his Boys Harbor was concerned with ghetto victims because "their anger and suspicion, if not reversed by proper education, can easily turn to the idear of communist revolution." Is the revolutionary overthrow of their own class, then, the thing that, at bottom, these patrician do-gooders are so worried about? Whatever the answer, there's no doubt that the Drexel Biddle Dukes are as up to their ears in the class struggle as any communist. Their telephones ring day and night, like the phones in a Red Cross crisis center.

Again the phone . . . "Hello Mother. Yes, the King of Morocco? How interesting! How very *in*teresting! I'll tell him that. I'm going to see him at dinner tonight. Yes, yes, I'll take it from there, now that you've warmed the matter up. Okay? God bless . . ."

Plutocrats of the world, unite! You have nothing to lose but your marble palaces.

Author with John Hay Whitney at Belmont Park

John Hay Whitney winning Belmont Stakes, with sister, Joan Whitney Payson

U.S.S. L.S.T. 530
Anthony D. Duke, *Lt. Comdr.* — Commanding

Author aboard Boys Harbor boat with "Tony" and Mrs. Duke and boys

Author at home of Mr. and Mrs. Anthony Drexel Duke

Chit-chatting of an afternoon with Mrs. Cordelia Drexel Biddle Duke

Ambassador Angier Biddle Duke with his ambassadorial flag

FOUR

1
A War-Within-A-War

In the late 1930's, I was vehemently opposed to the foreign policy of the U.S. Government. What progressive person, let alone communist, wouldn't have been? Indeed, the foreign policy of the American ruling class in the late 1930s only proved that Karl Marx was right in saying that the capitalist class is interested in democracy only to the extent that it doesn't interfere with their profits. When it does, that class won't hesitate to crush democracy, as it did in Italy with Mussolini in 1922, in Germany with Hitler in 1933, and in Spain with Franco in 1939.

The democratic Republic of Spain, for instance, was under attack by enemies of democracy in 1936-39, and the U.S., to say nothing of Britain and France, lifted not a finger in its aid. Hitler, with the cooperation of Mussolini, was, in fact, permitted to deliver the *coup de grace* to the Spanish Republic with the tacit approval of the Western democracies. That was because the Western capitalist class had bigger fish to fry. Abandoning the left-liberal Spanish democracy to the fascists might encourage Hitler to turn East and liquidate the hated Soviet Union, something the capitalist class the world over dreamed of ever since the 1917 Russian Revolution, when Winston Churchill declared: "The communist infant must be strangled in its cradle."

So, on a world scale, the battle lines were drawn, not between "democracy and dictatorship," as the Western ruling classes, in need of cannon fodder for their imperialist wars, would have their people believe. Rather, it was a contest between a moribund capitalist system dependent on recurrent war to solve its economic problems, and a youthful socialist alternative committed to economic democracy.

Then, on June 22, 1941, Adolph Hitler, fulfilling his historic anti-communist mission, invaded the Soviet Union, and the character of World War II changed. Now it was something more than the usual imperialist war between capitalist powers for control of profitable markets. Now it was also, and more importantly, a war to determine whether mankind was to continue having, in the example of the Soviet Union as the only existing socialist state, a model for human society other than profit-bent capitalism. And when, later that year, the Japanese ruling class bombed Pearl Harbor, and the war became all-out, I decided that, no matter what the motives of the capitalist powers in their odd alliance with the USSR, my place was in the ranks of the anti-fascists.

"I'm joining up," I informed my wife. "My place is in the army with the rest of the citizenry."

"You crazy?" she said. "You supported Republican Spain against Franco's fascists when it was considered 'premature' to be anti-fascist. You backed the Russians in the Soviet-Finnish war when the capitalist press was screaming: 'Poor little Finland!' With that kind of record they'll assign you to latrine duty."

"But both Franco and 'Poor little Finland' wound up supporting Hitler. So I was prematurely right, wasn't I?"

"So much the worse for you, then. A two-bit Marxist right and the capitalist press wrong? If they allow you in as an officers' boot-polisher it'll be a miracle."

Nevertheless, I was determined to join the army. Being a pragmatist as well as a Marxist I decide to enlist at Baltimore, where I was still a member of the bar. This would open possibility of service as a photographer, my then-occupation. Or it might mean assignment as a lawyer (I was also a licensed attorney) perhaps in the Judge-Advocate Division, and possibly Military Government later. Even more, it might mean basic training near my home town.

When I inform the recruiting sergeant of my dual professions he reacts as though he had won the Irish Sweepstakes. With a military caught so short of experienced personnel by the Japanese surprise attack, it is a feather in the cap of a recruiter to turn up a man who has a potential for special assignments.

"Just what we're looking for!" exclaims the gravel-voiced Regular Army man. "Photographer *and* lawyer! Perfect combo for Counter-Intelligence!"

Remembering my wife's admonition ("with that background it'll be a miracle if they even let you in") I hardly have time to swallow the shock of "Counter-Intelligence," that word so dreaded by communists, before the sergeant has me on my way to G-2, the intelligence division, with a sealed letter addressed to a Major Edmund L. Babbery 3d.

The headquarters of G-2, First Army Corps, Baltimore, Maryland, does little to relieve my uneasiness. Its being based in the local headquarters of Standard Oil Company, an entity which, even as far back as then, I considered one of mankind's mortal enemies, is itself enough to give me the willies. On top of that, the freshly-processed 2nd lieutenants, who occupy desks around the open "bullpen," all look like clones of J. Edgar Hoover's 100% American male. Blue-eyed, most of them, immaculately-shaven, with the quarter-inch of crewcut on their heads running a range of blond to a little-less-than-blond, they don't seem like anybody that a "subversive" would relish being left alone with in an interrogation room. *What am I doing here*? I mumble under my breath.

And yet, as I sit waiting with that sealed letter I slowly convince myself that it can't be all that bad. We're all Americans in the same boat, battling the same enemy. In any war it's necessary to gather intelligence, and all citizens, radical or conservative, must work together. My job would be to gather intelligence.

Major Edmund L. Babbery 3d, Harvard Business School graduate, stifles a cigarette, solemnly flicks an accidental smudge of ash from the miniature American flag on his desk, and smiles quizzically on reading my sealed letter.

"You've volunteered, I see," he says. "Counter-Intelligence is a dangerous business, sometimes more so than infantry. You prepared for that?"

"Yes, sir. I'm prepared to undertake any assignment for which my Fatherland thinks I'm fit."

"Then let's get to a few question." He straightens in his chair and fixes pale-blue eyes on me. "Are you a member of the Communist Party?"

What's that got to do with fighting a war against fascism comes out of my mouth as "No sir," even though the "sir" is gratuitous. After all, the man is obviously several years my junior and, as I am not yet officially inducted, he's not entitled to be sirred.

"Ever been one?"

"Never." (The truth, actually: I'd been a fellow-traveller but not, at the time, a Party member.)

"Ever been interested in Marxism?"

"I once had a go at *Das Kapital*," I say with a sardonic smile, trying to avoid seeming overly-innocent. "I suppose you couldn't get past the first ten pages, either, huh?"

He deflects my attempt at humor with a male version of the inscrutable Mona Lisa smile. "You're a lawyer I see. Ever defend labor unions in your practice?"

"No sir," I reply, considering it politic to continue sirring, as I was rapidly getting the feeling of being interviewed for membership in Hitler's *der Sturmabteilung* instead of an army at war with fascism. "There was little call for lawyers during the Depression. I gave up practice and became a photographer instead."

Seeming disappointed, as though, waging his own little war-within-a-war, he'd lost a battle to unearth an underground communist, the Major proceeds routinely down a list of questions which concludes with: "Are you a member of the German-American Bund?" That, and whether I'm a fascist sympathizer, seems not to interest him, for the former question he passes over as hardly important and the latter he doesn't even bother to ask.

"OK," he sums up. "Here's the deal. Assuming you pass the physical, you'll take thirteen weeks basic training. You'll be requisitioned back here, given a master sergeant's rating and, in plainclothes, head up an anti-sabotage photo-unit. Acceptable?"

"Oh fine, yes sir!" I exclaim. "Nothing I'd like better. I can be of great service at that sort of thing."

"Well then, here's what you do," he says, taking from his desk drawer a matchbox-size camera and a batch of blank report forms. "This surveillance camera—teach yourself to use it clandestinely. And these reports—you're to fill them out weekly while in basic training, and mail them to the address indicated. This is to be done in strictest secrecy. You are to keep eyes and ears open. Nobody, not even your company commander, is to know that you are to be assigned to counter-Intelligence. Otherwise your country and even your own life might be endangered. Got it?"

"Yes sir!" I say, snapping to, like a veteran infantryman.

My physical examination places me in limited service, that is, in non-combat category because of third degree *pes planus*: flat feet. But that hardly matters. A "flatfoot" is what my Fatherland wants me to be: a cop, a counterspy in plainclothes, and that's what I'll be. Moreover, my training camp is near my parents' home in Baltimore—at Edgewood Arsenal, where the U.S. Army Chemical Warfare Department manufactures poison gas. Could a soldier with third degree flat feet ask for a more exciting assignment?

So great, indeed, is my enthusiasm for this spy career that, in the week before induction, I gobble up tomes such as *How To Write In Invisible Ink*, *How to Look Two Ways At Once*, and *How To Be And Not To Be—Seen*. By the time I master the art of sitting in bars and looking as though I'm lighting a cigarette, while actually I'm aiming a secret camera, I am in a state of near-euphoria.

Except for one thing: those weekly reports that Major Babbery has ordered me to file. They require that I keep eyes and ears on my fellow-soldiers, particularly on those who talk communism or "other red subversion." I am also to keep watch for "outside" reds who try to propagandize, and for "labor agitators." At the bottom of the list, almost as an afterthought, as with Babbery's question about the German-American Bund, there is a suggestion that I report "anything else I think amiss." These weekly reports on the army's "little war-within-a-war" are to be mailed regularly to SMALL LOANS, BOX 1142, ELLICOTT CITY, MD., which is stamped on provided envelopes.

It makes me fume. Who is the nation fighting? Reds? Red Russia? Or anti-red Germany, Japan and Italy? How are American soldiers to confront nazi regiments if they are expected to hate the same thing that the nazis hate, that is, reds? Is this the Fatherland my immigrant grandfather had taught me to respect? Is this the army whose playing of the Star Spangled Banner had so thrilled me as a child at Francis Scott Key's shrine in Baltimore? I decide to fight my own little war-within-a-war and see what happens.

2
A Red Aroma

"NOW READ THIS," says a leaflet on the barracks bulletin board as I head for the shower one night in the second week of basic training. Pausing to cooperate, I read.

"While true Americans are in the military dying for their country, Abie Cohen and his ilk are sitting home getting rich. They corner the black market, they deal in counterfeit ration stamps, they grab the tires and gasoline your families must do without."

"Isn't it time that true Americans did something about it? Write home to your loved ones, who must already be feeling the pinch, and tell them the truth. Spread the message about Abie Cohen, wherever you happen to be. And remember, if you're lucky enough to come back from this war, DON'T FORGET WHO STARTED IT, SO THEY COULD STAY HOME AND GET RICH! Then make sure and do something about it yourself."

(Signed) TRUE AMERICANS FOR FREEDOM & JUSTICE.

I gasp, not because of the leaflet's content, but because it hangs there untouched by non-commissioned officers who pass the barracks bulletin board several times a day. And indeed I recall having also seen the same leaflet on the Day Room bulletin board when I arrived at the camp. Exhausted from the tension of being ushered in the army, however, I hadn't bothered to read the text. But there the scurrilous leaflet had hung—and in the Day Room, no less, which all the company's non-coms and, occasionally, even commissioned officers visited!

Yet, why so surprised? This is still very much the *lumpen* Regular Army, whose hero is the ultra-rightwing Douglas MacArthur, the kind of army that did not balk at executing his orders to drive veteran World War I bonus marchers out of Washington with fixed bayonets. My own unit is non-commed by fearsome Regulars named Ludwig and Muller and Streicher, whose innuendo I had already heard directed at draftees named Goldberg and Ginsberg and Cohen. I look around to see if anyone is watching, and, seeing none, rip the scrufulous leaflet off the barracks bulletin board and head for the shower room to flush it down the toilet.

Later that night I sit in the crowded Day Room, and, not daring, as I had in the barracks, to rip the leaflet off its bulletin board, stare at it in frustration.

It is time to file my second report. The previous week, having observed no "red subversion" or indeed "anything else I thought amiss," I had taken the chance of having my gung-ho *gauleiter* back at the Standard Oil Building consider *me* amiss, and simply filed "nothing to report."

But now I feel I indeed have something amiss to report. If you want agitators spreading subversion, here, with the NOW READ THIS leaflet, you have it with a vengeance. Whoever its "true American" authors are—Ku Klux Klan, German-American Bund, whatever—their message obviously will not encourage American soldiers to fight nazis who, in Europe, are taking care of the same kind of traitor that, in America, "stays home to get rich while others fight the war." I record these observations in my report, including the not-too-subtle allusions of Ludwig, Muller, Streicher & Co., post it to SMALL LOANS, INC., BOX 1142, ELLICOTT CITY, MD., and hurry off to my bunk.

The tenth week of basic training my wife shows up at Edgewood Arsenal on a visitor's pass. She has camp-followed me and found a job as designer in a Baltimore fashion house. We sit in the Day Room. The Abie Cohen leaflet still hangs on the bulletin board, but I tell her nothing of my report. She is nervous enough as it is about how the army will accept my "background." Besides, under Major Babbery's injunction, my work is strictly secret, even to my wife.

"They're investigating you," she whispers. "I didn't dare write."

"Who's investigating?" I whisper back.

"Army Intelligence. At least that's what the man said. He was in plainclothes. Blue-eyed with close-cropped blond hair."

"One of my future G-2 buddies at Standard Oil, I'll bet."

"What?"

"Nothing . . . What did he ask?"

"What clubs you belonged to. Who your closest friends were. Were you active in politics? And all the time he kept peering over my shoulder at the bookshelves."

"Bookshelves? You brought our books down from New York?"

"You said you were going to be stationed in Baltimore, didn't you? I'm here for the duration. But one thing," and here she glances anxiously around, "one thing he kept pushing. He wanted to know if you were religious, if you were militant about anti-Semitism. He kept asking the same question in different ways. I didn't get the point at all."

"Neither do I," I say, even though I now suspect that his anti-Semitism inquisition is possibly related to the Abie-Cohen report I had filed.

"And then he showed me a photograph. It was of you! Wearing a beret! Where could he possibly have gotten it?"

"From the New York Police Red Squad, probably. I was in lots of demonstrations to protest the arms embargo on Republican Spain. So what?"

"But he asked why, if you weren't French or Spanish you'd want to wear a beret?"

"You're kidding!"

"No, no! He said Americans didn't wear berets, and did your wearing one have a special meaning? All this investigating is making me nervous. He even showed up at my sister's to ask about *me*! I'm on pins and needles."

"Now, now—don't use that expression," I say, taking her hand and chuckling. "*Pins and Needles* is the name of that labor union musical revue. In this 'democratic' army, any connection with the workingclass is considered subversive."

Next morning, Sunday morning, my entire company is called out to a special shape-up for the company commander. There isn't a black face among the one hundred men on the mustering-ground.

"Ah don't know which of you were ovah in the niggah area last night," bellows Captain Truscott, mounted on an empty beer barrel, his Southern accent thick as lard. "And Ah'm not goin' to ask."

"Negro area?" I whisper to the trainee next to me. "What's he talking about?"

"Coon's quarters," he mutters back. "Some of us got loaded from that barrel Truscott's standing on. Had us a ball smashing up the jigs' Day Room."

"That is, Ah'm not goin' to ask this *first* time," continues the Captain. "Y'all new here. Ah know how y'all feel and Ah feel the same way. They're grumblin' 'bout segregation, they're grumblin' 'bout unequal treatment, and some politicians beginnin' to take up the cause. But Ah'm tellin' you, y'all stay out of it. It's leadership's job and we know how to handle it."

"You mean they have black soldiers segregated here?" I whisper to my informant.

"Yep. In a barracks up behind the mustard gas plant," he replies. "They might be in the army, but I wouldn't exactly call 'em soldiers. They're cooks and flunkeys for the brass."

"Y'all want to live it up on Saturday night," the Captain goes on, "find yourself somethin' else than startin' a riot. We got a war to fight. There'll be plenty of time to take care of domestic problems after we've won this war. Now this is an ordah! Niggah area is off limits. Ah don't want evah again to heah of this company goin' ovah there. Dismissed!"

I realized, of course, that the U.S. Regular Army was still a feudal institution. Black soldiers had always, except in wartime, been relegated to the kind of menial job they performed on the old plantations. And even in wartime they were usually formed into all-black, segregated regiments.

But to hear, at this late date and in this particular war, such blatant racism openly expressed in an official order by a U.S. Army company commander, came as something of a shock. Its very openness suggested that racism was accepted, though unofficial, army policy.

Or could it be that this incident represented only the personal philosophy of this particular redneck in a captain's uniform—his own little war-within-a-war? Whichever, I still considered it an insult to the ideas for which the nation was supposed to be fighting. And, despite the fact that my Abie Cohen report might well have been the cause of Blue-eyes-from-G-2's visit to my wife, I intended to report this new "something amiss."

Besides, as Major Babbery had assured me, even my company commander is ignorant of my being an intelligence operative, so that, were Captain Truscott disciplined for the race-riot, he would have no reason to suspect it was I who had informed. That night I mail my tenth report, nine previous of which—except the Abie Cohen—have simply stated "nothing to report." For the truth is that, despite spying overtime, I have observed no "communist subversion," no "labor agitators," nor anything else particularly "amiss."

Later that week, Captain Truscott calls me into his office. Sitting stiffbacked in his chair, he tries to stare me down, as nazi judge, Herman Goering, tried to stare down communist defendant, Georgi Dimitrov, at the Reichstag fire trial.

"Livingston, Ah know what your assignment is," he says. "so give it to me straight."

Uh-aw, this is the test, my baptism of fire. Major Babbery is probing to see if I am able to keep a stiff upper lip. "I don't understand, sir," I say, trying to stare *him* down.

"Ah'm privy to what y'all are heah for, Ah said," he repeats sternly.

"I'm sorry, sir, but I haven't the vaguest idea of what you mean."

"OK, stop the pussyfootin' and take this," he snaps, handing me a slip of paper. "A six-hour pass to see Major Babbery in Baltimore. Y'all be back at the post at six-hundred hours."

It doesn't require six hours to find out how I have done on my "test." Major Edmund L. Babbery 3d gives me a pretty fair idea in just about ten minutes. No mention of my Abie Cohen report, nor my Truscott racist-slurs report, nor even the eight other nothing-to-report reports. "You're concerning yourself with the wrong things." I had expected him to say. But no, nothing like that.

"Why didn't you tell me about yourself?" the Major says, instead—in a kind of hurt tone, like a man whose protege has turned out a disappointment.

"How do you mean, sir?"

"There's a red aroma about you."

"Red aroma?" I repeat solemnly, too stunned to react to the comic overtones of that expression.

"There seems to be an association with red causes. You should have levelled with me."

"But, Major, I answered all your questions about communism. And every word I uttered was truth."

"Words tell one kind of truth. But you and I know, soldier, that words can be used to conceal the truth. You seem to have been involved in some, shall we say, questionable things."

"Could you mean my signing a petition to protest the arms embargo against Republican Spain?" I reply, wondering if it is really possible that, in democratic America, such information can wind up with an Army major sitting at a desk in the Standard Oil Building.

"I'm not saying. You tell me."

"But hundreds of us signed such petitions at college. Does it make us communist to petition our democracy to aid another democracy that's fighting for its life? You never asked me about Spain, and I certainly didn't think it necessary to 'confess' petitioning my Congressman. It was my way of fighting the fascism we're all now fighting."

"In 1937 our government wasn't fighting fascism. Maybe you were a bit premature. At any rate the War Department says definitely no to your counter-intelligence assignment."

"But why?"

"That's confidential."

3
Closet Commissar

Latrine duty! With basic training over and that red aroma exuding from me, latrine duty is what I expect for the duration. And latrine duty is pretty close to what I get. Assigned to a photo-processing lab at Edgewood Arsenal eight hours a day in dungeon darkness, I develop pictures in chemical solutions which assail my nostrils like odors from an overused men's room. Captain Truscott, True Americans for Freedom & Justice, Major Edmund L. Babbery 3d, had all won their little wars-within-a-war. And I am now fighting fascism in a photographic darkroom.

One morning, after several weeks in this hellhole, Lt. Colonel Norman E. Niles, commander of my unit, the Training Aids Division of the Chemical Warfare Department, which produces technical manuals, films and other media for training in poison gas warfare, opens the door. I rub my eyes at the sudden entry of white light, come to attention and salute.

"Livingston."

"Yes sir?"

"Be in my office in a half hour."

My God! I mutter, as I resume swishing prints in the slimy

fixing bath. The Colonel himself coming for me! What heinous crime have I committed now? I literally sweat perspiration into the fixing bath as I anxiously count the minutes to the next half hour.

"I'm taking you out of the darkroom and assigning you to an administrative job," says the Colonel, putting me at ease in his office. "You'll be my assistant, with responsibility for checking out confidential correspondence before it gets to me."

My jaw drops.

"I'm also putting you in for a master sergeant's rating," he continues. "You'll have ten men under you."

Is he crazy? Checking out confidential material! This must be a ruse to entrap me with secret material before I pass it on to the Russian enemy!

"You look surprised," he chuckles. "It is a big jump from private to master sergeant. But it's an important job and I need a man with your background. My old master sergeant was transferred to Washington."

My background! I'm still so stunned I can't do more than nod.

"Well, say something, Private-soon-to-be-Master-Sergeant Livingston," the Colonel says jovially. "We're not very military in this unit. Soon you'll be calling me Norman instead of Colonel. How do you feel about your new assignment?"

"Well, gee, Colonel," I reply, forcing a smile as I peer into the adjoining master sergeant's office I will occupy. "After the darkroom, this daylight office alone is more of a promotion than the master sergeant's six stripes. I accept your offer."

"Good," he says, shaking my hand warmly. "Move in this afternoon."

Next day I sit in my new office pouring over top secret documents on chemical warfare. It's unbelievable! Only a few weeks ago the War Department had detected an aroma on me which it considered "red" enough to foul up its G-2. Now there is a sign on the secret document safe that reads: EYES ONLY— LT. COLONEL NILES & M/SGT. LIVINGSTON. Even more unbelievable is my weekly assignment to pick up at the railroad station visiting foreign army officers—including Soviet officers—who make exchange visits to our Chemical Warfare School. How easily I could slip the red "enemy" our latest secrets!

Finally I fathom out what seems a plausible explanation for the mystery of my new assignment. Colonel Niles, I discover, had been a civilian photographer at Edgewood Arsenal before the war. Having seen war clouds on the horizon in 1938, he hastened to join the Officer Reserve Corps, so that by the time of Pearl Harbor he was already three leaps ahead of new officer material. This advantage, plus the fact that he had been a civilian photographer experienced in chemical warfare, got him appointed Lt. Colonel and head of the newly-created Chemical Warfare Training Aids Division.

But, having spent his entire life in Magnolia, Maryland, a metropolis of some three hundred souls not far from Edgewood Arsenal, he was not exactly a model of self-confidence in the world of higher brass. So much so, in fact, that, when he received complicated communications from higher authority in Washington, he often fell to biting his nails over how properly to compose a businesslike reply.

It was my guess, therefore, that when he discovered in my file that I was a lawyer, he concluded that he had found someone who could respond to Washington's epistolary gobbledegook without compromising him. My New York City flair would also be useful, he felt, in helping him cope with his provinciality, which I had already observed in his dealing with bigtime Hollywood movie people who came to Edgewood to film for the army. In addition, my being a non-commissioned officer meant that he could exploit my assets for his personal benefit, and still, should he so choose, keep me at a social as well as professional distance.

So much for why Colonel Norma E. Niles would want me as an aide-de-camp. As to why my G-2 file had not caught up with me to preclude such possibility I had no answer. The only reason I could conceive, was that it had to do with the same root cause which made possible U.S. entertainment of Japanese diplomats in the White House even while Tokyo's bombers were on the way to Pearl Harbor. In short, the right hand of the U.S. Army often knew not what its left hand was doing. Slovenly management somewhere along the line, I figured, had aborted my file's journey from one military department to another.

At any rate here I sit, in a sunny office, a closet communist giving orders not only to army civilian employees who have been certified as anti-communist, but also to the ten God-fearing soldiers under me. A jeep is at my disposal. I can authorize trips for myself to Baltimore photosupply houses to purchase supplies for Training Aids. I have unlimited access at the PX to personal goodies rationed in the city. I don't even have to bother sirring junior commissioned officers, as I had prematurely sirred Major Babbery. The only thing I have to fear is not fear itself, but rather the slim chance that Major Babbery might sniff a red aroma as I airly plummet an army jeep through Baltimore with six stripes on my arm. And all of this country-club existence, not because of the Fatherland's gratitude for volunteering my service, but because of a shy Lt. Colonel's insecurity. For the moment I forget about the shabbiness with which this ungrateful Fatherland has treated me. Especially is this so when the army approves my request, as a married non-com, to live in Baltimore City with my wife.

4
Victory

"Let's try that one," says my wife, seeing an apartment-for-rent sign on a Federal-period house as we drive through an old section of Baltimore. A plaque mounted on the front reads 1798, testifying to the landmark's hoary age.

"Do you think we should?" I reply hesitatingly. "I know this area well. It's Daughters of the American Revolution territory. Aristocratic old Baltimore families who've fallen on hard times have lived here since the Revolution, and they're angry about having to let out rooms."

"I heard that Scott and Zelda Fitzgerald lived here, so it can't be that awful. Besides, it looked clean and quiet."

"OK, we'll give it a whirl."

We park the Army jeep, climb the footworn marble steps and ring an antique, wrought-iron doorbell. A wait of five minutes and the exquisitely-carved oaken door creakily opens. Out of the dim light emerges a venerable female face wearing a

95

Victorian-age hat crowned with a fully-plumaged stuffed bird. The bird trembles with its owner's arthritic movements as though preening its feathers.

"Yeeeees?" she says, drawing out the word as she looks us over.

"My wife and I would like to see the apartment."

"Well, come along inside, won't you," she replies, leading us into a darkish room off the hallway. "I'll prepare some tea. Make yourselves comfortable. I'll only be a moment."

Velvet-portiered, Persian-rugged and lit by a ten-watt bulb in an electrified old Tiffany chandelier, the room resembles a Gold-Rush San Francisco bordello. We slink warily around in the dim light like patrons trying to find seats in a dark theater. Finally we discover an overstuffed davenport with a dislodged spring which, as I sit on it, elevates my left buttock. Our hostess's "moment" has extended to ten, when suddenly a white light flicks on and she reappears wearing a Spanish shawl festooned with a brood of birds that look like relatives of the one who nests on her hat. She sets out a service of tea and settles into a chair beside us.

"I'm Mrs. Parran," she announces, handing each of us a dainty china cup in a manner suggesting that we'd been formally invited to lunch. "What, may I ask, is yours?"

"Livingston. Sergeant and Mrs. Livingston."

"Oh, a fine old name," she says, reaching for a book on a table beside her. "It goes back to the Court of St. James. I'm president of the Maryland Genealogical Society. Do you know your family crest?"

"Well . . ."

"Yes, yes," she mumbles, impatiently flipping through the dusty pages. "Here it is. It consists of a demi-savage, wreathed round the head and waist with laurel, holding in his right hand a club, and in the left a serpent, which is twisted about his arm."

"My own forbears," I reply, shooting a sardonic glance at my wife, "left Livingston Manor in New York sometime around 1810 to trade furs with Russians in Alaska. They found it politic in dealing with the Russians to change their name from Livingston to Litvinski. So our coat of arms got a bit mixed up. But when they came east again in 1920 they took back the old name of Livingston. We . . ."

"They should never have relinquished it. Robert Livingston signed the Declaration, you know."

"Yes," I reply, continuing the charade, "My cousin's great-great-great grandmother was married to Robert's second cousin, a van Rennselaer. But we never see much of the van Rennselaer branch of our family."

"Well, Sergeant, you and your wife may certainly have the apartment, if you like. We have a few other respectable guests staying with us, and we'd be happy to have you join us."

Since housing in wartime Baltimore is hard to find, we sign the lease for the tiny, one-room so-called apartment, despite the fact that there are onerous stipulations. Felt slippers must be worn when walking across the floor (there is no rug); no talking in the hallways ("This is *not* a rooming house"); visitors must ring the single doorbell the number of times assigned to each resident guest ("There are no separate guest door bells to degrade this *private* residence").

That night we move in. Having gone through our initial

inspection of the "apartment" so cursorily, we had failed to inquire about kitchen facilities. Now we discover that the "kitchen" is a Woolworth two-burner electric hotplate mounted on the inside of the door to the toilet, an arrangement which conveniently enables you, when you close the door, to stir the simmering stew while you do your business on the john. The bathroom is a stall of corrugated metal that, when the shower hits it, makes a noise like sound-effects for thunder. And heat is a tired whiff of warm air which piffs every now-and-then from a grate in the floor.

Not to be discouraged. We grit our teeth, bring in dinner from a nearby Chinese restaurant, shower at the YMCA and sleep in army longjohns under our landlady's paper-thin blankets. My wife also tries to arrange the furnishings in a style more to her personal taste. Next morning, after I leave for Edgewood Arsenal, she changes the pictures on the wall, moves the rickety furniture around and adds a touch of bright fabric to the deathly-dull sofa.

The same day I come home early to check on my wife, who had nearly frozen to death the night before, even though we had slept in longjohns and piled our overcoats on top of the blankets. She is still trembling. I insist that we immediately go downstairs and complain about the lack of heat.

"But Sergeant," says Mrs. Parran, "you must pull the window shades down. The shades keep the heat in."

"What heat?" bellows my wife. "There's no heat to keep in! I've been home all day and haven't felt a drop of heat."

"Young lady, lower your voice, please. There are other guests in the house."

"Indeed there are. They're all half-frozen to death. But they're too frightened of you to complain."

Our elegant landlady draws herself up in shock.

"Why, Sergeant," she gasps, "your wife must be a Jew! To go soliciting my guests! This is a restricted neighborhood. I'll not have a Jew in my house."

"Did you hear that?" my wife screams into the hallway, ignoring the injunction against talking there. "There's a Jew in the house! A real, live New York *Jewwww* in the house!"

Doors on the upper floors suddenly slam tight as the eaves-dropping guests dart back into their rooms. Mrs. Parran slumps into a chair, the stuffed bird on her hat trembling violently.

"I'll not have a Jew in my house, Sergeant," she repeats. "Besides, your wife is indefatigable. She's presumed with my effects, re-arranged my furniture and pictures, made a shambles of the apartment. You're a gentleman. But your wife . . . You must leave this house at once!"

Mrs. Olive Peabody Smith, around the corner in another old townhouse that accepted "guests," was forthright when, evicted by the President of the Maryland Genealogical Society, we inquire in advance about *her* policy on religion, namely, that of Jews.

"I certainly would accept Jews if any applied," states the genteel Baltimore Daughter of the American Revolution, "but I definitely don't approve of marriage with Negroes."

At first I am loath to risk how she might get along with my wife, who, though Caucasian, has a darkish complexion and kinky hair. But, having found no other vacancy, I decide to let Mrs. Smith's views on racial intermarriage go unchallenged. At least she didn't ask, as did everyone else: "Are you now or have you ever been a member of the Communist Party?"

Like frowsy Mrs. Parran with her bird hat, the stylishly-coiffed member of the declassed old Baltimore ruling class refuses to acknowledge that she harbors commercial tenants, and insists, too, on having a single doorbell for all her roomers. Also, like her neighbor's, Mrs. Smith's mansion has aristocratically gone to seed. Except for one thing: a magnificent white marble staircase leading to upper floors and remindful of earlier days of upperclass splendor—the only component of the house, in fact, which still has loving care lavished on it.

And each morning as my wife, with her off-color skin and Africanish hair, descends this gleaming monument, Mrs. Smith peers from an adjacent doorway as though she has never seen her like.

"I hope you don't mind my asking, Mrs. Livingston," she finally ventures. "You hair . . . what is it that Jewish women use on their hair?"

"You mean what dressing we Jewesses apply to our beautiful tresses?" replies my wife, caressing her kinks in mock self-admiration.

"Yes. Is it Richard Hudnut or Elizabeth Arden or any of the preparations we women use?"

"Oh horrors no, none of those, Mrs. Smith. Chicken fat. Didn't you know that Jewish women are forbidden to use anything on their hair but kosher chicken fat?"

Following this incident we find freshly-carved swastikas on our window sill and complain to Mrs. Smith, only to have her tsk-tsk: "Oh, that Michael Cressup! I don't know what to do about my errant son. He's not in the army, he doesn't work in the war plants. I just don't know what it is he does."

But I do. Michael Cressup Smith is probably a member of TRUE AMERICANS FOR FREEDOM AND JUSTICE, and the kind of "outside agitator" whom Major Babbery's little war-within-a-war on the homefront intended that I should disregard. Next day my wife and I move out of the genteel Mrs. Smith's mansion and lodge with my parents in their shabby two-family house in the Baltimore suburbs.

But I was not to escape the homefront war so easily. One afternoon, as I was about to leave Edgewood Arsenal for the day, Colonel Niles invites me into his office.

"I want to talk to you abut something, Bernie," he says, closing the door with an onimous gesture. "Sit down."

"What is it, Norman?" I ask nervously.

"You and I are going to be in a secret organization," he announces, moving a batch of blank report forms to the center of his desk.

"Secret organization?"

"A counter-intelligence setup," he says, patting the packet of papers.

"But what is it? I don't understand."

He goes to the door, opens it and checks carefully up and down the corridor.

"Reds," he says, returning to his desk. "We've got to keep eyes and ears open for communists. You among the enlisted men, I among the officers. We've got to listen to what they talk about."

"That's spying, Colonel," I say with a straight face.

"That's snooping on our buddies."

"I know, Bernie. I feel the same way. But it's got to be done."

"But isn't that an enormous waste of our precious time? Our unit is way behind on every project as it is. Just this morning we got a message from a colonel on Guadalcanal who said that by the time our training manuals on chemical warfare reach his troops they're already obsolete and the men could better use some good toilet paper. I mean why should we devote time to hunting reds?"

"Sure I realize. But it's got to be done. It's a directive from Washington."

"So why choose me?"

"You're the best qualified for the job."

Before I know it my hand is raised in reluctant oath. I am inducted as a member of the Edgewood Arsenal Counter-Intelligence Unit and I have thrust at me a packet of papers with self-addressed envelopes that read: SMALL LOANS, BOX 1142, ELLICOTT CITY, MD. To my consternation I am back again in the Fatherland's little war-within-a-war.

Being by this time a hardened veteran, however—at least a veteran in the homefront war—I simply ignore the whole business, even to the point of not sending in a single report for fear that Major Babbery might see my name and catch up with me. The little war is made even more poignant one morning when Colonel Niles informs me that one of our newest officers, a Captain Ernest Moorer, has been summarily restricted to quarters, and that I am to intercept his mail.

The Captain, a marvelously gung-ho officer, who seemed anxious to tear at the fascist enemy with his bare hands, early on had been a reserve officer like Colonel Niles. The War Department had urgently solicited him to accept an active assignment, and when he revealed that he had been a correspondent for the communist *Daily Worker*, had responded, "What's the difference? We're all fighting the same war, aren't we?"

By the time he reached Edgewood Arsenal to write technical manuals on chemical warfare, some eager-beaver red-hunter in Washington apparently saw the possibility of "red subversion" creeping into literature on the use of poison gas and pulled him off the job. Or was it Colonel Niles himself who, perhaps having overheard Captain Moorer being overly-enthusiastic about the Soviet victory at Stalingrad, had done the axe-job? Whichever, Captain Moorer was decomissioned faster than you could say J. Edgar Hoover.

Next came myself. In August 1943, the Army decided to have another look at my flat feet.

"We're going to discharge you for the convenience of the Government, Sergeant," says the medical officer. "You've got third degree *pes planus*."

"I've always had flat feet, sir," I reply. "Even when I plodded those ten-mile training marches with equipment on my back. But the U.S. Army is not going to brand me with any ambiguous 'convenience of the government discharge.' If you want me out, it's honorable discharge for physical disability. Else I'll petition Wendell Wilkie to fight my case."

Mr. Wilkie having notably and successfully taken up defense of civil rights for political dissidents, the threat must have had some weight. For, quicker than you could say Major Edmund L. Babbery 3d, I am ready to be processed through honorable discharge by way of a final interview. But even there, agents of the ruling class try to make sure no closet communist escapes undetected in their little war-within-a-war.

"I see by your file that your grandparents were born in Russia," says the close-cropped, blond-haired young nazi in the three-piece civilian suit. "How do you feel about Russia?"

"I like borscht, and Rubinoff and his violin," I reply, looking the man I might have been, had the army accepted me for G-2, squarely in his blue eyes.

And I answer in the same flippant way each of his tricky questions that are based on data in my file. Finally he despairs of tripping me and pursues another tack.

"Got any hobbies?"

"None I can think of."

"What about music? You said you like, uh, what's his name . . .?"

"Rubinoff. Rubinoff and his Russian gypsy violin."

"Paul Robeson," he snaps back like a whip. "Did you hear Paul Robeson sing in Druid Hill Park last night?"

"How did G-2 know Robeson sang in Baltimore last night?" I said, smiling. "I didn't know."

As I matter of fact I did. I even attended the concert, over my wife's objection that I was in uniform. I simply informed her that SMALL LOANS, BOX 1142, ELLICOTT, MD., expected me to spy on my fellow soldiers, and that—nothing else—was why I would do such an unpatriotic thing as go to hear Paul Robeson sing. I had even shaken the man's hand. He too would one day be having trouble with his Fatherland.

FIVE

Five Easy Pieces—
A Rulingclassic Whoretorio

All the ruling class had to show for my twenty months in its army was (1) a record of my third degree flat feet, and (2) a file on the red aroma which despoiled my otherwise 100%-American aura.

That's all the ruling class got. But I—I got a new profession. In 1943, with most of their staff photographers overseas as war correspondents, the big international newsphoto services, such as AP, INP and Acme, were desperate for domestic photographers. As a consequence, on discharge from the army, I, even with my third degree flat feet, easily landed a job as staff photographer for the New York Bureau of Acme Newspictures. There, in five easy pieces, I learned a thing or two about "free" capitalist enterprise.

PIECE ONE: PRELUDE

Acme Newspictures is a plum of a job. Great proving ground. It spawned some of the world's greatest camera artists.

Margaret Bourke-White cut her photographic teeth there. As did Weegee "The Famous," so-named because of a mental Ouija board that supposedly endowed him with a precognition which enabled him to scoop the competition.

Great listening post too. Acme photographers assigned to the White House, Ten Downing Street, the Quai d'Orsai and other sanctuaries for capitalist obfuscation of the news, would assemble on occasional sabbatical in the New York bureau to pass the poop they regularly observed but were never permitted to photograph. We heard inside stories about Madame Chiang kai-Chek's wartime visit to the White House and her subsequent departure with two planeloads of Parker 51 fountain pens, which later appeared on the Chinese black market; we learned of J. Edgar Hoover's low profile with "companion" Clyde Tolson at posh watering-places where pictures were either forbidden, or, if taken, never found their way to the public press; we savored FDR's foul language when he got into those terrible iron leg-braces for stand-up pictures; we cracked up over pintsized Tom Dewey's insistence, during his Presidential campaign against Truman, on being seated on telephone books when photographed at his desk.

And a power base too—what unexpected and inappropriate power! Is there anything like the infelicitous leverage of the capitalist press, particularly the news photographers? On my first Acme assignment, Eleanor Roosevelt's arrival at the Waldorf Astoria for a speech, I see photographic pipsqueaks who, though they probably couldn't conjugate the verb "to do," pack enough clout with their cameras and press cards to order America's First Lady around for pictures as though she were a child. One of them, chutzpah king, Sammy Shulman of Hearst's International

News Photos, is actually addressing Mrs. Roosevelt as "Mamma," and getting away with it! Am I too, a closet red, *really* a member of this noble order of the capitalist Free Press?

PIECE TWO: TWILIGHT SERENADE
Variations on a National Anthem

Oh say, can you see
Any bedbugs on me?
If you do, pick 'em off
By the twilight's last gleaming.

This is how the teenage Babe Ruth, along with other young "delinquents," mischievously parodied the national anthem at his Baltimore reform school's annual patriotic festivities.

But now, at the Bankers Trust Company Victory Bond Rally in New York, 1943, when the nation was in the midst of a life-and-death war, the legendary Babe was doing no such thing. No siree! The old King of Swat wasn't singing at all when, on my second Acme assignment, I arrived at the rally in the last gleaming of a cold December twilight. He couldn't. If the beloved Bambino, now wasted by creeping cancer, could have raised his voice he'd surely have belted out the real national anthem, as did the crowd of passersby attracted into the bank by his presence.

This was a patriotic rally. Bankers Trust, like most other big New York banks, was keeping its doors open well after twilight to sell war bonds in support of the war against the nazis and Japan. And this was just another on the bank's long list of bond rallies. Its public relations department had dragged the Bambino from his sickbed to autograph free baseballs for bond buyers. Serious business. Babe Ruth wasn't singing any of that "bedbugs on me" nonsense this time. Neither were the bank's employees. Neither was I. It was, for me, a war against fascism, even if, for many of my countrymen, it was only a national war against Japan, Germany and Italy, with the Soviet Union oddly thrown in as a more-or-less unwelcome ally.

"Hi, Babe, I'm an ex-Baltimorean like you," I say, trying to cheer up my boyhood hero, now being relentlessly consumed by the poison of numberless nitrite-filled hot dogs he'd devoured over forty junk-food years. "My father took me to Baltimore Stadium every time you played for the Orioles. Man, how I loved to see you belt those homers out!"

"Jeez, that's great." The voice is scratchy-gravel, eyes heavy-lidded with pain, focusing on the press card in my lapel.

"I'm from Acme Newspictures," I proudly say, trying to impress the Babe with my fourth-estate importance.

"Yeah, I can see from your press card. Jeez, I didn't think the press was still interested in me."

"You must be kidding, Babe, You're the greatest. Can I get a shot of you autographing a baseball?"

The emaciated old warhorse moves painfully toward the huge silver bowl which contains hundreds of new Spauldings. Memory takes me back to a scene of that lumpy, potbellied figure circumnavigating the four bases after a colossal swat which sends a roar over Yankee Stadium. Babe would wave to the bleachers and clasp his pudgy hands over his head in the victory salute. Pandemonium!

Now, he scrawls an arthritic signature over a pristine base-ball and hands it to a wide-eyed child, whose father is the rally's first bond buyer. As a cheer rises to the vaulted ceiling, I flash my first picture: Babe, child, father, and, of course, Bankers Trust branch manager, whom Frank Baer, my Acme editor, has instructed me to be sure to include in the group. The Bambino smiles. A job well done. He has patriotically crawled out of his sickbed—no charge at all—to do his part in the battle against Hitler, Tojo and Mussolini. And Jeez, just like in the old days, the press is here into the bargain.

I, for one, however, see no other press on the scene. What's the reason, I wonder? Oh well, there's probably a good reason. Maybe the war: shortages of photographers and materials—all that. Perhaps my pictures will be used in a pool by all the news services. Although I pride myself on a sophistica-tion worthy of a communist in a capitalist society, I'm still too green in this business to know the answers.

Meantime, while I flash away, the exhausted Bambino swats out I don't know how may thousands of dollars in Victory Bonds, before twilight's last gleaming yields to winter night at Bankers Trust and the crowd goes home to dinner.

In the taxi, after the rally is over, the press contact, a Bank-ers Trust p.r. man, is tired and a little drunk.

"I'll be glad (hiccup) when we're finished with these bond binges," he burps.

"Me too. It'll mean the war's finally won."

"Tha's not what I mean. It's these goddam late hours. Th'

bank volunteers our after-hours services to th' Treasury Depar-'men'."

"Well, I think that's admirable. I mean, the bank donating its premises, its employees, and all that. I never realized that banks were so patriotic."

"Oh, didn't you?" replies the gin-relaxed flack. "Well, I'll let you in on a li'l secret, m'boy. Our wunnerful patriotic bankos are indeed workin' overtime for th' war effort, employees' time contributed free. (Hiccup) Know why? 'Cause they've got 'nun-nerstandin' thith U.S. Treasury to realize one p'cent profit on all the money they hannle. Now les' see. How much is one p'cent of a billion dollars? Why, jus' a mere ten million. And tha' doesn' include the discount they get on the Spaulding baseballs, either. Tha's our great patriotic bankos' patriotism."

"Okay. That's not hard for me to buy. But what about Babe Ruth? He seemed to think the rally was a legitimate news event that the general press was covering. Why was I there exclusive?"

"Guess you're new 'n th' job, huh? (Hic) Acme was *hired* to shoot pictures for us, m'boy. Have camera, will travel. The li'l ole Babe doesn' know it, but the only press his photos will ever see is our bank's newsletter. 'S important our employees be shown what a grea-ayt patriotic job their employer's doin'. (Hic) Tell Frank Baer I wanna see prints by tomorrow noon."

So that's why I had an "exclusive!" This so-called news event is a phony. A ripoff. Poor Babe was used just to make a buck for Bankers Trust. I arrive on the scene, announce myself as coming from Acme Newspictures, but I'm actually there to shoot photos for the bank and get the famous Babe into the picture. I feel like an FBI stoolpigeon posing as a legitimate newsman.

"Ya wanna be noncommercial, go to Russia and work for Tass," snipes Frank Baer, Acme Special Services editor, when, returning from manipulating the Babe, I complain that the assignment was a for-hire job and not an authentic news coverage. "Whaddaya here, two days? Well, ya better learn fast that Acme Special Services For Hire is the department that keeps Acme News goin'. The News Department don't produce nuthin' but red ink."

"I thought I was supposed to be a photo-journalist. You assigned me an Acme press card. But I'm shooting pictures as though I work for some commercial photo studio."

"An' if you worked for Associated Press, Hearst, Scripps, anybody, you'd be doin' likewise. The *New York Times* even has a commercial portrait studio. Everybody's got commercial departments for hire. Wheredaya think the real buck is?"

"But it's a fraud selling a news service for hire."

"Like I said," repeated Baer, "ya wanna turn in your press card and go noncommercial, I hear *Pravda* is lookin' for some good men."

Oh say, can you see any bedbugs on me?

PIECE THREE: MARCHÉ MILITAIRE

"WITH AMERICAN TROOPS SOMEWHERE IN NEW GUINEA, Dec. 11 (Delayed) (Ap)—After 23 days of attacking through New Guinea jungles and swamps against a Japanese foe determined to resist to the last man, American and Australian forces still have a formidable task . . ."

"Livingston," Frank Baer calls out as I sit reading the AP teletype in the Acme Special Services Department while awaiting my next assignment. "Do me a favor. Take this into the News Department and give it to teletype, will ya?"

I pick up the memo he hands me and read:
XYZ 75494 ACME SPECSERV NY BUR FB
TO ACME WAR CORR., US ARMY, NEW GUINEA
SHOOT SIX NEGS ESSO SMOKE GENERATOR IN
BATTLE ACTION. MUST BE DRAMATIC SHOW
UNIFORMED SOLDIERS SUITABLE ESSO ANNUAL
REPORT LAYOUT.
"You're kidding of course, Frank. It's a gag, huh?"
"Gag? Waddaya mean?"

"I mean you're actually asking the Acme war correspondent in New Guinea to take out time covering the most decisive action of the war to make commercial pictures of a smoke generator for Standard Oil?"

"Fer Chrissake whatinhell's a-matter with you? Esso's got to get out its annual report. You think they want their stockholders to see that Shell or Texaco equipment is doin' a better job in the war?"

"And not only to shoot six pictures, but also get fighting men to pose with Esso's product. I suppose Acme's war correspondent will remember to get signed releases from the soldiers, won't he?"

"Nah, we won't need no releases. He'll shoot the faces in profile. Acme photographers know better'n to show identifiable faces in commercial pictures."

PIECE FOUR:
SELECTION FROM "THE GREAT MOGUL"
Opera buffa

GRAND CENTRAL STATION, NYC, 1944. The Twentieth Century Limited pulls in. Red carpet is rolled out, passengers detrain. A short sun-tanned man, important-looking in custom-made shoes, black Homburg and otter-collared greatcoat, steps out of the Pullman car. His manicured nails glint in the gleaming lights.

Four photographers with Speed Graphic cameras rush up. "Hold it, sir! Look this way please!" the cameramen flash bulbs, change film-holders in rapid sequence. The short sun-tanned man smiles as he deliberately shifts stance for each shot. "One more, sir!" the lensmen plead. "Can you wave your hand?" The Homburged man complies. The shooting finished, the highly-pleased subject walks off, followed by a safari of Pullman porters carrying expensive luggage.

"Who was that guy?" I ask Mike, senior of the three other Acme men who, along with me, have been flashing bulbs like mad.

"Shit, I don't know," he replies. "Some big mogul from

113

Warner Brothers, Hollywood. Larry Bolub, Warner's New York p.r. guy, hired Acme to send us down here."

"But we must have flashed off fifty bulbs and we didn't have a single sheet of film in our cameras."

"Right. Warner's is one of Acme's biggest commercial clients, and this guy is a bigshot from their Hollywood operation that Larry's got to brown-nose. So he asked Frank Baer to send us down here and flash off a lot of bulbs. Makes the guy feel important and Larry look good, like he was able to get the New York press to cover his arrival. The guy thinks he's being shot by the *Times, News, Trib* and all the rest."

"But what when he looks for his pictures in tomorrow's papers and finds nothing?"

"Aaah! By that time he's forgotten all about it. And if he asks, Larry's got a million excuses till the next time. Come on, let's get back to the office for the next load of shit."

PIECE FIVE:
SELECTION FROM "NABISCO"
Opera Seria

WALDORF-ASTORIA HOTEL, NEW YORK CITY, 1945. The Grand Ballroom is packed to overflowing. VIP's out in force, newsmen all over the place. But somehow it's shivery, as though somebody has returned from the grave. Up there on the dais, gaunt in his four-star general's uniform, battle ribbons covering half his shrunken torso, Jonathan M. Wainwright, who left fifty pounds of his flesh in Japanese prisons, sits, a ghost reincarnated.

The war over, the nation is grateful to the point of tears. Guilt-ridden, almost, about this giant who made the Bataan Death March uncomplainingly, while most of us sat it out at home in comfort. No corn-cob pipe protruding from his mouth like MacArthur, no elegant tailor-made uniforms, no wading theatrically onto Pacific beaches with photographers in attendance. Asking of his captors, in his four-year prison stint, nothing more than that granted the lowliest private. Many in the Grand Ballrom are weeping even now.

The General pokes slowly at his food: his mouth not yet accustomed to heavy fare. Speeches are made, testimonials. The Cardinal, the Bishop, the Rabbi perform their amenities. And now the General.

Photographers arrange groups of VIP's around the hero. Dozens of cameras flash, including those of Acme News Department, all of which this time are loaded with film. It's a big, *authentic* news event. The General finds it hard to smile. "One more please, sir." Fatigue overtakes his face as he tries to cooperate: "Smile, General. Give us a smile." He spreads his thin lips. The cameramen, settling for that, flash their last bulbs. And now his speech. The speech of a soldier: short, humble, to the point. Lincoln at Gettysburg. Three minutes it's done, he's back in his chair on the dais.

And I, yes even I, an emissary of Acme Special-Services-For-Hire Department, with an authentic press card on my lapel, have made my way up on the dais to approach the General. Before he departs I too have an amenity to perform. In my camera case there's a box of Nabisco crackers.

"Acme Newspictures, General," I announce. "I'd like to get a *special* picture."

"Yes?" he inquires patiently (after all, I, ostensibly, am the press). "What is it you'd like?"

"Acme Newspictures services hundreds of small-town newspapers with pictures. Could I shoot you doing something homey, say, like munching on a cracker. It's the kind of photo the country weeklies like."

"Well, I suppose so," the hero of Corregidor replies, looking around on his dinner table for a cracker to accommodate.

"Here, General, I have a cracker," I say, taking one from the Nabisco package that all Acme Special-Services-For-Hire photographers carry in their cases.

The General obediently munches on the Nabisco as I flash my bulbs. As had other celebrities innocently puffed cigars, drunk Cokes, sucked Lifesavers, all conveniently provided by Acme Special Services for Hire photographers for other "news" pictures. A front page photo of Jonathan M. Wainwright nibbling a Nabisco cracker! Can you imagine what National Biscuit Company would pay for that? *Fer Chrissake, wheredya think the big buck is*?

But this is Jonathan Wainwright, who must often have hungered even for a cracker during those four cruel years in prison, not some dizzy Hollywood starlet who'd strip in Macy's window for a full-page spread in the *Daily New*. Shit on National Biscuit Company! Or whoever else will give Acme and its photographers a bonus for a picture of Jonathan Wainwright munching a cracker! To hell with the Cigar Institute, Coca Cola,

Lifesavers or any of the other Big Business celebrity-picture buyers! Not even for the duPont Nylon Rope Company, which I'm sure would have hired Acme to shoot pictures of their rope around Hitler's neck, had he been hanged, would I ever again say, "One more please!"

And shame on you too, Bernard Livingston, a communist committed to fighting for a decent world, that, no matter how urgent your need for a job, you allowed yourself, even for a moment, to whore for the capitalist "free" press!

Five easy pieces—a rulingclass whoretorio . . . *Wheredya think the big buck is*? This fifth piece was enough to make me slip into the Waldorf-Astoria men's room and flush my Wainwright-munching-a-cracker negatives down the toilet.

SIX

Penetrating A Rulingclass Hype Tank

1
Class-conscious Delivery Boy

It's four o'clock of a summer day in 1958, and I'm replenishing the chewing-gum-and-candy display at the cashier's counter in the Hotel Warwick Coffee Shop in New York. It's the first day of the four-to-midnight shift on my new job as a cashier, cigar clerk, and delivery "boy." A far cry from photographing presidents and generals for Acme Newspictures, and a big comedown from award-winning documentary film producer.

But, the new television medium having emerged on the scene, documentary film producers were now a dime a dozen, and the competition for film contracts overwhelming. Particularly for me. The ghost of McCarthyism still haunted the broadcast networks. Government film contracts were out of the question (during my Acme service, an application for overseas employment as Office of War Information photographer had been rejected by the Government on "ideological grounds"). The old red aroma still hung over me. What they were so afraid

119

of in this war against the fascists, I still couldn't quite comprehend.

At any rate, I settle for the only job I can get: cashier for fifty dollars a week and such tips as I might earn as an overage delivery boy for outgoing orders. At least, I congratulate myself, thinking of the Hotel Warwick pot roast special that comes free with the job, I'm spared my wife's soybean concoctions, to which my two years of unemployment has once again reduced us. It's not unthinkable, really, to go on indefinitely like this. Fifty sure bucks a week, nice hot pot roast specials every night, including free Alka Seltzer for the resulting heartburn. No more sniffing around for indulgences from the ruling class. No more having to hide my true self for the sake of bourgeois success. From here on it's a charmed life of days spent with Mozart and Marx, Freud and Lenin, and the simple pleasure of being privileged to walk this lovely planet. It's sheer euphoria!

That is, until the day a certain press agent pays his luncheon check at the Hotel Warwick Coffee shop, and then hands me ten dollars for some expensive cigars.

"What are you doing here?" asks the beefy flack, beading me with puffy eyes as he pokes a dollar Churchill Premium into his mouth.

"Enjoying a life of serving achievers like you," I reply, flicking a match to light him up.

"You don't remember me, eh?"

"Should I?"

"I once had you on a photo assignment. You worked for Acme Special Services, right?"

"Right."

"Twelve years ago I was with General Foods as a p.r. man. Don't you remember the publicity pictures you took of kids at Henry Street Settlement House baking a cake with one of General Foods' cake mixes?"

"Yes, sure I do."

"And I asked you to place the black kids on the fringes of the group so we could crop them out when we printed the pictures? Mixing black kids with whites in an advertising photo wouldn't sell our products in the South . . ."

"My God, Hal Windbreaker! You were a lean and hungry guy then. No wonder I didn't recognize you."

"Prosperity," he says, tapping his ample gut. "Got my own p.r. shop now. But you were right, you know, refusing to put those black kids on the end of the group."

"Oh, I was just being contrary."

"No, it took guts to risk your job that way. Now, of course, with all this civil rights crap, things are changed. I always insist on including at least one nigger—I mean black—in any group picture. But what are you doing here? Setting up for some p.r. pictures?"

"Nope. Joe McCarthy, with his un-American crap, got me and things changed. I fell on hard times and had to give up the picture business. Now I'm a real, honest-to-goodness coffee-shop cashier and delivery boy."

"You're kidding! A guy like you doing this crap? Why don't you quit and try your hand in the p.r. world. It's a cinch."

I smile as he steps aside to help a handsome black woman put on her mink coat, and let her pay the check.

"I'm happy here, Hal. No grief. I've cut back on my ambition. I go home every night in peace to enjoy life."

"Don't hand me that. Once the excitement bug has bitten you, you're hooked. You just mark time till the next shot. When I got dumped at General Foods, I spent a whole year peddling insurance. Dullsville! Man, it hurts to see a guy with guts like you wasting his potential."

"But suppose I did want to take a crack at p.r., which I by no means imply, I've no samples of p.r. work to show a prospective employer."

"Forget it. I'll lend you a sample portfolio. You can put your name on it and say you worked for me. The p.r. business is all hype and soap-bubbles. Any kid with half a brain can do it. Here," he said, producing a gold-embossed Gucci wallet, "take my card. Give me a blast when you make up your mind."

2
Closet Red As Corporate Flack

It took two weeks and much soul-searching before I concluded that self-abnegation for a worthier life was for more hardy souls than I. This decision was expedited by my wife's observation: "Self-abnegate for yourself all you want, but who the hell are you to decree the same for me, even if you do bring home a Warwick pot roast special occasionally?" What she wanted, she made plain, was an occasional Twenty-One Club *poulet amandine a l'orange*. And, as for Mozart and Marx, Freud and Lenin, fine and dandy, but sipping martinis with Jock

Whitney in his box at Saratoga Racetrack, while watching Capot swoop across the finish line wouldn't be all that painful, either.

In the end I succumbed. The kind of high excitement which had characterized my previous exploits among the high and mighty, much of which had spilled over into my wife's life, could as easily be abnegated as Abbott could abnegate Costello. "Once the excitement bug had bitten . . ." as Hal Windbreaker had said . . . And he was right. In a matter of days I had his faked p.r. portfolio in my hands with a phony resume to match. Then I noticed a charming little ad in the *Times*.

> MAN'GT CONS. SEEKS P.R.
> DIR.
> WI GEN EXP. FINE OPPTY.
> EQU OPP EMP. HI SAL.
> PHONE TJDG TE 9-8500

Getting back into my clandestine communist garb, I telephoned TE 9-8500 to renew my lifelong career as "red" mole burrowing in the capitalist pasture.

"This portfolio is damned impressive," observes John Diebold, president of TJDG, The John Diebold Group, management consultants, in his mahogany-panelled office at 40 Wall Street. John, as the nervous young tycoon with an angry facial rash insists I address him, walks tall among autographed portraits of Alfred Krupp, Axel Wenner-Gren, Paul Getty and others of his monopoly-capitalist clients that decorate the walls. "Did you write all these articles yourself?"

"Of course, why do you think they're in my portfolio," I shamefacedly lie, this time wearing no French beret to brand me as a dissident to the rulingclass Establishment.

"Yes, yes, then sell me on why you want this position," he says, removing his Savile Row jacket to roll up elegantly-cuffed shirtsleeves and open a can of wax polish.

"I didn't even know, until I looked in the telephone directory, that you were a MAN'GT CONS," I reply, mimicking his abbreviational *Times* ad. "But I *am* a P.R. DIR. And I do have WI GEN EXP. All I ask is a FINE OPPTY. And, of course, a HI SAL."

John Diebold, as he hand-polishes his prize Queen Anne mahogany table with Johnson's Wax, cracks not a smile at my mimicry which I hoped might tickle him enough to hand me the job outright. And I say to myself, Uh-aw, here goes this FINE OPPTY with a HI SAL down the drain.

"Well, well," he says solemnly, "you didn't bother to research us, check out our clients, prepare a pitch on why you want to work for The John Diebold Group?"

"There wasn't time. I saw the ad only yesterday."

"Uh-huh, uh-huh. Then you'll have to take our psychological test."

"What's that?"

"We have a psychologist test job applicants so we can decide if we want them to work for us."

"I'd be delighted to take your psychological test on one condition," I reply, convinced that, what-the-hell, this job is already caput. "And that is, if you'll take *my* psychological test to determine if I want to work for *you*."

"I like you, I like you!" he exclaims, smiling for the first time. "Forget about the test. You've got style. Can you start tomorrow, Bernie?"

"Yes, sir. And I'd rather you called me Bernard, not Bernie. How'd you like me to call you Johnnie?"

"Right, right," he agrees, wiping the wax from his hand to shake mine. "As to salary—since I advertised HI SAL," he said, now grinning broadly, "I'm giving you the top: TEN THOU."

"Thanks, John. You really *are* an EQU OPP EMP."

Next morning, under orders to spend a week learning what The John Diebold Group is all about, I settle into my office. This consists of an 8′x10′ glass-partitioned cubicle that I share, practically back-to-back, with two staff management consultants. A single phone, which we all lunge for when it rings, serves to keep the three of us in touch with the outside world. My title, I'm told, is director of public relations, and an elegant embossed card is being printed up to officialize it. But just exactly whom I am to direct is not apparent. I'm aware of no assistant who is to report to me, nor even of a secretary to take dictation. Public relations *director*? It seems that, like those one-man businesses which call themselves such-and-such associates, I am the entire public relations department.

Nevertheless, despite the one-man p.r. operation, The John Diebold Group itself is certainly no one-man affair. There are dozens of people out in the "bullpen" poring over paperwork. And there's a goodsized stenographers pool, with an impressive array of copying machines, office appliances, charts and bulletin boards. Not a second seems wasted: people buzz away, as though racing against a stopwatch. Twice this morning a tall, blonde, baby-faced man with an angry facial rash, catapulted out of an office at the front of the bullpen and whizzed down the corridor, body slanted 45-degrees forward, while simultaneously, issuing from an office at the back, a tall, bony, grim-faced woman slanted 45 degrees forward zoomed toward the front. As the two went by each other, slanted in opposite directions, their passing bodies formed a momentary triangle. They spoke not, neither did they smile: they could well have been ships passing in the night, not Mr. and Mrs. John Diebold, president and vice-president, respectively, of The John Diebold Group, international management consultants who offer FINE OPPTYS WITH HI SAL. to P.R. Dirs such as myself. Such, in this place, seems to be the obsessive concern for speed, get-on-with-it, and performance.

Gradually, as the morning wears on, I begin to get a picture of what and whom, as p.r. director, I am expected to publicize. At age twenty-eight, I learn from back files, John Diebold is already being referred to as the "elder statesman" of automation. This came about as a result of his having written, at the tender age of twenty-four, a dissertation entitled *Automation: The Advent of the Automatic Factory*, in which he was said to have dropped the "tiza" from automatization to coin the new word automation.

Once out of college young John, with that fiery evangelism which was to give him the angry facial rash and characterize his meteoric rise to eminence, lost no time in bringing his message to public attention, aided largely by efforts of a young publicist of equal grasp and drive, named William Safire. John had a golden voice, a baby face and a gift for Harvard Business School gobbledygook that mesmerized corporate executives who were terrified by the mysteries of the new electronic data processing technology. With the mantle of his newly-coined word around his shoulders and a reputation as a kind of young Mozart of the new management science, he had no problem infiltrating Griffenhagen & Associates, an oldline, Chicago-based management consultant firm. There, as fast as grant took Richmond, John took Griffenhagen and became its sole owner.

From that vantage point, always stressing the fact that it was he who had coined the magic word automation, he merged and acquired, acquired and merged, until soon he captained a worldwide string of management consultant firms specializing in automation. Now, all he had to do was to appear at some international businessmen's convention with a black Homburg on his blonde young head, mumble gibberish about closed-loop, economic contraction, Cobol, realtime, and frightened industrialists would come flying, checkbooks in hand, to commission automation studies to rescue their facilities from obsolescence. The impecunious college boy-wonder was now dictating correspondence in a chauffeured Rolls Royce as he scooted from conference to conference across Manhattan. He was also making business deals while riding horseback with tycoons in Palm Springs, and receiving regular midnight calls from Swedish billionaire, Axel Wenner-Gren.

Not only, at 33, was he self-designated the "elder statesman" of automation, he was also the "efficiency expert" of the world. And all because he claimed to have coined a single word. (Enoch J. Haga, however, in contradicting that claim states, in *Understanding Automation*, 1965, that "For over 100 years, from 1649 to 1751, the word 'automate' was in currency. It then became obsolete until our own generation, when the suffix *ion* was added . . . More than one individual has claimed or been credited with its resurrection. But, alas, never has one word meant so much to so many!"). I could see now what Hal Windbreaker meant when he said p.r. was pure hype. And to my increasing horror, I, with a phony portfolio, had taken on the job of hyping for this "ninety-day wonder" of Big Business.

Well, it was a job. I hadn't had a pair of new shoes in years and my only business suit was getting frayed. I decided to try and cover up my utter lack of experience in p.r. and hang on long enough at TJDG to accumulate a reserve. The thing to do was to shoot for something big, a *tour de force*. Perhaps plant a profile of John Diebold, high priest of automation, in *Fortune, Business Week* or *The New Yorker*. In the world of capitalism, those were the plums of the p.r. world; if I could arrange such a coup, I could write my own ticket. So I settled in.

"You through with the phone soon?" I ask management consultant A, my cubicle-mate with a hacking cigarette cough. He is busy picking some engineer's brain over the wire.

"I'm waiting for it," interjects consultant B, my other cubicle-mate, who has been patiently picking his nose for the past fifteen minutes.

"Good God, I've been here over a week now," I reply, "and I've had only two cracks at the phone. How do you guys ever get any business done?"

"You plan your time for use of the phone," says B. "John wants it that way."

"In my job you can't plan time. You're at the mercy of media editors. They're hard enough to reach as it is."

"John says that a shared phone makes for a more efficient use of time."

"Well, what about the phone in John's Rolls-Royce? Whom does he share that with? His chauffeur?"

"John is different. He's in the public eye. He needs a private phone in the Rolls for his image."

"Yes? Well, I'm trying to build his image by getting the editor of *Business Week* on the phone. Maybe I'd do better by sending smoke signals."

Consultant B goes back to work on his right nostril, while I, following the Diebold guideline for maximum efficiency, resume my research in the interval between the next telephone availability.

I find nothing on John Diebold in *Who's Who in America* for 1958. But that hardly makes a difference. As his p.r. representative *I* am supposed to be his *Who's Who*. I select the best quotes from his newspaper clippings, underline the high-sounding jargon in his speeches, have him photographed dictating like a Cardinal in his Rolls-Royce, compose a glowing portrait of his rise from damp-behind-the-ears acolyte to world-shaking high priest, and wait for a chance to sell all this hype to *Business Week,* over the phone.

(*Note*: Twenty years later, in 1979, long after I'd left him, I thought about young John Diebold again and, for kicks, looked him up in the current *Who's Who in America*. Wouldn't you know! There he was with an entry of twelve inches! Longer than anyone under the D's, including public figures of such stature as Justice William O. Douglas, General James Doolittle and Ambassador Angier Biddle Duke. I hadn't the patience to check through the rest of the alphabet but I had a sneaking suspicion that, with the honorary degrees which the boy-wonder had gleaned from a host of second-rate colleges in addition to memberships he holds on all kinds of undefinable committees, his entry was the longest in all of *Who's Who*. Certainly it was longer than Henry Kissinger's, Richard Nixon's and Jimmy Carter's.

DIEBOLD, JOHN, bus. exec.: b. Weehawken, N.J., June 8, 1926; s. William and Rose (Theurer) d.; B.S. (Regtl. Acad. award) U.S. Mcht. Marine Acad., 1946; B.A. with high honors in Econs., Swarthmore Coll., 1949; M.B.A. with distinction, Harvard, 1951; LL.D. (hon.), Rollins Coll., 1965; Sc.D. (hon.), Clarkson Coll, 1965; D. Engring. (hon.) Neward Coll. Engring, 1970; L.H.D. Canaan Coll., 1972; D. Comml. Sci, (hon.), Manhattan Coll., 1973; m. Doris Hackett, Nov. 22, 1951; 1 dau. Joan. With Griffenhagen & Assos., mgmt. cons., N.Y.C., also Chgo., 1951-57, owner, 1957-60, merged with Louis J. Kroeger & Assos. to become Griffenhagen-Kroeger, Inc., 1960; chmn. bd. Griffenhagen-Kroeger, Inc. 1960—; founder Diebold Group, Inc., mgmt. cons. N.Y.C., 1954, pres, chmn. bd. 1954—; founder, Diebold Europe S.A., 1958, chmn. bd. 1958—; founder, chmn. bd. Mgmt. Sci. Tng. Inst., 1958—; founder John Diebold Inc., mgmt. and investment, 1967, chmn. 1967—; DCL Inc., holding co. of Diebold Computer Leasing, Inc., 1947—, chmn. Gemini Computer Systems, Inc. 1968—. dir. Genesco, 1959—. Mem. Sec. Labor Adv. Com. Manpower and Automation, 1962-66, Pres. Kennedy's Com, Dept. Labor's 50th Anniversary, 1963; mem. U.S. delegation UN Sci. Conf., Geneva, Switzerland, 1963; mem. adv. council Soc. for Technol. Advancement of Modern Man, Switzerland. 1963-76, mem. com. human values Soc. Advancing Tech. Nat. Council Chs.; 1965-74; mem. nat. adv. council Peace Corps, 1965-70; mem. Com. on 2nd Regional Plan for N.Y.C., 1966—; trustee, sec. Bus. Council for Internat. Understanding, 1970—; mem. Internat. Inst. Strategic Studies, London, 1971—; bd. consultants, mem. adv. com. UN We Believe, 1972—; mem, Adv. Council on Japan-U.S. Econ. Relations, 1972-74; mem. steering com. Atlantic Conf., 1972; mem. Council on Fgn. Relations, 1967; mem. adv. group developing fgn. affairs program, planning and budgeting system sec. state, 1966-67. Chmn. vis. com. Sch. Bus. Administra, Clarkson Coll. Tech, 1961-66; vice chmn. vis. com. econs. Harvard, 1963-69, 70—, mem. vis. com. engring, and applied physics, 1974—, adv.

council Inst. for Crippled and Disabled N.Y.C., 1957—; mem. U.S. adv. com. European Inst. Bus. Administrn. 1965—; mem. bus. adv. com. Grad. Sch. Indst. Administrn, 1965—; mem. bus. adv. com. Grad. Sch. Indst. Administrn., Carnegie-Mellon U., 1969—; trustee Freedom House, 1969—, Com. for Econ Devel, 1970—; vice chrmn. Am. Council on Germany, 1970—; founder, pres. Diebold Inst. Pub. Policy Studies, 1967—; trustee Carnegie Instn. Washington, 1975—; trustee, vice chmn., legislation com. N.Y. Met Reference and Research Library Agy. 1974—; mem. com. for African industrialization Club de Dakar, Paris, 1973—; pub. mem. Hudson Inst., 1967—; mem. vis. com. Center for Research in Computing Tech and Office for Info. Tech., Harvard, 1971—, mem organizing com. on Harvard and East Asia, 1974—; mem. adv. council Grad Sch. Bus. Administrn, Columbia U., 1968—; mem. vis. com. Grade Sch. Mgmt, Vanderbilt U., 1971—; bd, dirs. Acad. for Ednl. Devel. 1972—; trustee, mem. exec. com. Council of Ams., 1971-74; trustee Nat. Planning Assn., 1973—; founding mem. mem. exec. com. council Rockefeller U., 1973—; mem. adv. com. ethical and human values of sci. and tech. NSF, 1973—, indst. panel on sci. and tech, 1974—; trustee Overseas Devel. Council, 1974—; mem. Nat. Acad. Sci. Evaluation Panel for Oversight over Inst. Computer Scis. and Tech., Nat. Bur. Standards, 1975—; mem. N.Y. Gov.'s Planning Commn. for Conf. on Libraries, 1976—; N.Y. Sheriff's Jury, 1967—; Served with USNR, World War II. Decorated grand officer Order of Istiglal (Jordan); grand cross Eloy Alfaro Pound. (Panama); grand cross Order St. Martin (Vienna); commendatore Order Merit (Italy); Order Merit (Germany). Named one of ten outstanding young men U.S. Jr. C. of C., 1962. Fellow J. Pierpont Morgan Library, 1973—; Mem. Internat. Cybernetics Assn. (dir. 1957—), AAAS (sect. com. on indsl. sci.), Am. Printing History Ass., U.S.C. of C. (council on trends and perspectives 1969—), Internat. C. of C. (trustee U.S. council 1971-74), Center for Inter Am. Relations, Mid-Atlantic Club N.Y., Author's Guild (com. on the 70's, 1970-73). Clubs: Harvard Business

School, Economic, Union League, Harvard (N.Y.C.); Metropolitan (Washington); Chicago; Bohemian (San Francisco); Reform, Burkes (London). Author: Automation, The Advent of the Automatic Factory, 1952; Beyond Automation, 1964; Man and the Computer—Technology as an Agent of Social Change, 1969; Business Decisions and Technological Change, 1970; also articles. Editor: World of the Computer, 1973. Home: 1 East End Ave. New York City, N.Y. 10021 Office: 430 Park Ave. New York City, NY 10022.

"The phone's yours," announces Consultant A, after a full morning of arguing with someone in Rochester about "bugs" in a mysterious closed-loop system.

"Good!" I exclaim. "If John finds out I've been using the pay phone down in the lobby I'll get his latest lecture on efficiency and realtime. How long can I use this phone?"

"I'm expecting a call from Park's Pork Sausages." interjects Consultant B. "Don't tie it up too long. They're having problems with the automatic control panel for the sausage casings."

3
Bye Bye Wall Street

I had been at work now for two months, including the week I'd taken to acquaint myself with Diebold, his firm and accounts. And so far, nobody had the slightest suspicion of how I really felt about this bandit missionary for the capitalist class.

Moreover, I had acquitted myself not too badly at work. Accepting Hal Windbreaker's dictum that the p.r. business was mostly hype, I quickly learned how to plagiarize other people's work and managed to plant items in rather important publications. This despite the polygamous telephone, the crowd scene in my 8'x10' cubicle and the fact that I had to wait hours for a stenographer's pool to get a "rush" news release typed.

Now I wanted to consolidate my position by pulling off that long-planned *tour de force*: a profile of John Diebold in *Business Week*. I'd already made something of a coup a few days before, when Mr. and Mrs. D. came charging out of their respective offices at their accustomed 45-degree slant to inquire if anybody knew how to wangle complimentary tickets for the Arthur Godfrey Show. It seemed that a couple of important clients, who were in town with their wives, had decided at the last minute that they wanted to see Godfrey in person at the TV studio, and Diebold, with all his upperclass connections, couldn't come up with four tickets on such short notice. Playing a long shot, I yanked our overworked phone out of Consultant A's hand. After five minutes on the wire (Godfrey had once put himself in my debt by asking me to privately screen *Greentree Thoroughbred* for his friend, the monstrous General Curtis LeMay of "bombing-the-Vietnamese-back-to-the-Stone Age" fame). I was able to say, "There'll be four tickets in my name at the gate, John."

Now, I said to myself, *with a coup like this, perhaps, if not a private office, the p.r. director might at least be rewarded with an individual phone.* But nothing of the sort. Maximum efficiency was still the watchword. In order to get *Business Week* on the phone I still had to transport the instrument from Consultant

A's desk to my own and dial Editor Jerry Bock for the seventh time this week. To my surprise I finally got through.

"Jerry!" I practically bellow (a hypey p.r. man immediately goes on a first name basis, even if addressing Queen Elizabeth herself). "This is Bernard Livingston, p.r. director for The John Diebold Group. I guess you were away and couldn't return my calls."

"Yeah?"

"Jerry, John Diebold, as you no doubt know, coined the word automation . . ."

"Yeah, I know. Your predecessor unremittingly brought that to my attention."

"And he's also the youngest in the field . . ."

"Right. 'Elder statesman,' isn't it? And 'high priest'? But there's a whole Curia of high priests out there now. Peter Drucker, Norbert Weiner, Carl Kaysen. It's all you can do to keep count of them."

"No doubt, Jerry. But Diebold is unique in the automation field . . ."

"I'm sure. But we've got to go slow on all those rosy projections you guys make about the new technology. I hear there was a $4-million automated system installed at a Ford body plant, based on some feasibility study. On the first run the fenders came out as bumpers instead of fenders. Did John Diebold have anything to do with that?"

"Oh I shouldn't think so. As far as I know Ford is not one of our clients."

"Well anyway, what is it you have in mind?"

"A profile, Jerry, a success story. Whatever one might think of John Diebold personally, there's no doubt he's made a huge success. And I thought *Business Week* would be the right place to run a new version of the American Dream come true."

"Send me a presentation, some background, and let me kick it around. I'll get back to you."

The next six weeks was an ordeal of waiting. Public relations, particularly when devoted to hyping after the media, is the most chimerical of businesses, not like any of the professions I'd previously pursued. As a lawyer, you deal with tangibles: there's an issue, you make a case and, win or lose, there's a verdict. In photojournalism, again tangibles: even if your photos are never published it's the editor's responsibility, not yours—you've done your job in shooting the pictures. Documentary films even more so: *Greentree Thoroughbred* was a finished piece of work, and, had it never been shown to an audience other than John Hay Whitney and his upperclass friends, I'd have fully performed my function.

But spending weeks hyping after *Business Week* in hope of pushing John Diebold into a tenuous limelight was like plunging your life savings on a racehorse: pick wrong and you've not a thing to show for your effort. Public relations, or at least, Big Business p.r. as Hal Windbreaker had so honestly put it, was pure hype and soap bubbles.

Yet despite the hype and bubbles, publicity is the stuff of which careers are made. And even as I sit stewing in my over-populated office waiting for a call from Jerry Bock, I see an example of classic hype at the highest level. William Safire, John Diebold's former p.r. advisor at Tex McCrary, Inc., had just managed to push his client, Vice-President Richard Nixon, into an unscheduled "kitchen debate" with Nikita Khrushchev at a Moscow fair, a coup resulting in a story flashed around the world with unimaginable publicity for "tricky Dick." In a hype-manipulated society such as capitalist America, hype like this could catapult even a man who was "not a crook" into the U.S. Presidency.

Meantime, with only three months of actual p.r. experience under my belt, I'm functioning as an information channel for an organism that is reproducing itself each day like some bacterial mould. Out of a single nuclear germ, John Diebold & Associates, Inc., the Diebold virus of programmed automation has multiplied into a colony of voracious clones that simply embody exactly the same program in manifold different forms. There is, besides John Diebold, Inc., individually, The John Diebold Group, John Diebold & Associates, The Diebold Management Sciences Training Institute, Diebold Europe S.A., The Diebold Research Program, and, in the planning stages, John Diebold Investment Fund. Like the employment agency entrepreneurs who, in the 1950's came out of nowhere to interpose themselves as middlemen between the prospective employer and employee for a slice of the job-procuring fee, the Diebold organism seems hellbent to encrust itself over the entire electronic data processing pie.

And the disease is rapidly spreading through Europe. "Urwick Diebold Ltd. and Berenschot Diebold N.V. in Amsterdam are running on a profitable basis," John advises me by cable from London. "Activities in France are about to get under way. Italy is also doing well. But John Diebold & Associates Deutschland GmbH is also now a fact, with commitments from Ciba, Werner, and Krupp under way. Switzerland is next. For Germany a modern office is already furnished in a building at Kaiserstrasse 33 Frankfurt am Main." I set the cable aside, wondering how many inefficient hours it will take me to process it through the logjammed stenographers pool into a rush news release that boasts of John Diebold's European conquests.

"A specter is haunting Europe," I say to Consultant B, with a sardonic smile on my face.

"What?" he asks, throwing a quizzical look at Consultant A.

"A *specter* is haunting Europe . . ." I repeat, hardly able to contain my laughter.

"That's from the Communist Manifesto, isn't it?" says Consultant A.

"Oh, is *that* where I heard it?" I reply, even more sardonically. "I thought that, like automation, it was one of John's coinages." And I pick up our tired telephone, wondering if that "new modern office" at Kaiserstrasse 33, Frankfurt am Main, was doing any better with communications instruments than I. Or, indeed than Karl Marx had done with the overworked hand-powered printing press in the squalid office of the International Workingmen's Association in London.

Hardly have I released Diebold's cabled data to the business and automation media than he is back from abroad at his desk. And he's none the worse for his whirlwind invasion of the executive suites of Europe, except for a slight automation of the chronic rash on his face.

"What's holding up the *Business Week* story?" he demands as he works away at hand-polishing his Queen Anne table.

"It's been only six weeks since I presented it to Jerry Bock, John."

"I know, I know. Six weeks! I've wrapped up sixteen deals in six *days*. And I travelled to Rome, Munich, Cologne, Mainz,

Frankfurt, Zurich, Paris, Amsterdam, London and Glasgow. *Business Week* is just at the end of a local phone call."

"That's what I want to talk to you about."

"What, what?"

"What's at the end of a local phone call. John, you're supposed to be the efficiency expert of the world. What do you think Jerry Bock would say about efficiency if he knew that, at the end of a local phone call to John Diebold's p.r. spokesman, there are three men, one of whom has to win a karate bout to get at the single available instrument? It takes me more time to accomplish a local phone call than it took you to cover all of Europe. And that I do by going down to the lobby pay phone."

"Pay phone, pay phone? I hope you're not filing cash vouchers for those calls."

"Of course not. I know you'd countermand them."

He places the can of wax back in his desk drawer and smiles lovingly at his gleaming antique.

"Look, look," he says, "I polish my furniture myself. I shared a single phone for years, not with two but five men. And I still occasionally mimeograph my own letters."

"Goddammit, John, that's ancient history. You don't drive your own Rolls-Royce or cook your own lunch, do you? You spend I don't know how much on psychologically testing people to see if they're fit to work for you. You pay top dollar to hire executives away from Revlon and Alka Seltzer so these same people can go back to their contacts at Revlon and Alka Seltzer and get you consulting business. And you won't install a phone for your p.r. director so an editor doesn't hear a scuffle on the wire when he calls! I hope *Business Week* isn't thinking of automating, because when Jerry Bock phones me he might have to wait an hour to get through."

"You should call him. You should keep on top of Jerry Bock."

"You don't keep on top of an editor, John. That'll put you on the bottom of his shit list."

"And besides," continued the young man in custom-tailored British clothes, "your hair is too long. I'm partial to the English hair style, yes. But you're here at 40 Wall Street, not Fleet Street. It's not an appropriate business image."

On the twelfth day of my fifth month at TJDG, while waiting to have my English-style hair Wall-Street trimmed (it's 1958, remember), I'm using the barber's pay phone to talk to an editor at *Automation Magazine*. I'm trying to induce him to use an excerpt from an article on automation Diebold wrote for the National Planning Association in May 1958, in which he had guaranteed that the new automation technology would not cause unemployment.

"It is a matter of historical record," Diebold wrote, "that over a period of time there have been employment opportunities for those displaced by economic change . . . Some even doubt that any 'displaced' labor will develop. The rate at which the labor supply is increasing is not keeping pace with increases in the demand for labor. Within the next twenty years we will be facing not a labor surplus but a potential labor shortage. The demand for labor will in all probability exceed the supply . . ."

To my shame as a communist, however, I try to hype this bullshit onto a gullible public, when I know from every tenet of Marxism that "within the next twenty years," the U.S. would be facing not "a potential labor shortage," but in fact a huge labor surplus. And I wonder if those bourgeois economists who know the Marxist truth every bit as well as I, suffer the same pangs of guilt when, hoping to extend capitalism's life a few more years, they pass out the same rulingclass hogwash.

When I return to the office carrying an eat-in lunch (I'd used my regular lunch hour for the haircut, in deference to Diebold's policy on the efficient use of time) Consultant A, palming the phone's mouthpiece, informs me that *Business Week* had just called.

"What? Give me that phone!" I yell.

"But I'm talking to . . ."

"I don't give a damn if you're talking to Alexander Graham Bell!" I cry, yanking the instrument from his hand.

He yields, more out of surprise than docility, and I furiously dial Jerry Bock, only to get his secretary.

"Mr. Bock asked me to say that he tried three times to reach you this morning, but the phone was always busy," she informs me. "He left at noon for a meeting of the British Management Association in London, and he'll be abroad six weeks doing a series of articles."

"Didn't he leave a message concerning the Diebold profile for me?"

"Yes. He told me to tell you that next time he tries to contact John Diebold's p.r. department it will be by carrier pigeon."

I give the phone back to consultant A. Then I sit down and scratch out a letter.

Dear John:
Luv this fine oppty & hi sal. But wish no longer 2 b TJDG p.r.

dir. A man'gt cons firm like yours with 1 tel 4 3 men is no equ opp emp; 2 say so is misleading. The truth is that 2 him of the 3 who grabs first, goes the tel. The oppty is not equ. In cage by my desk have left carrier pigeon. Cons A can use 2 reach clients when Cons B is on the tel.
Sinc
B.L.

I bid goodbye to my buddies, Consultants A and B, and give the letter to the stenographers pool for typing, with instructions for routing it to the mahogany-panelled office. Then I go down to the lobby to phone my gratitude to Hal Windbreaker for having induced me to take a shot at public relations for the ruling class. It was a most edifying experience.

One day, many years later, 1985, I checked on how John Diebold was doing. Automation was going great guns, as he had prophesied in that 1958 National Planning Association article. Mechanical robots were taking over the factories, computers were an essential component of almost every important process. But there had *not* been, as the "high priest" had predicted in the National Planning Association article, "employment opportunities for those displaced by economic change." In 1985, as many as 10 million people were out of work in the United States.

John Diebold, however, was quite profitably employed. To all of the other myriad Diebold companies, he had added the DLC holding company for Diebold Computer Leasing, the (Diebold) Gemini Computer Systems, the Diebold Venture Capital Fund, the Diebold Institute for Public Policy Studies, the Diebold . . . the sharp-nosed hound who sniffs out super-profits opportunities for the capitalist ruling class was doing quite well, indeed.

Author as U.S. Army photographer in World War II

Author as UPI press photographer hamming it up with Sammy Shulman of INP (left) and Ken Lucas of AP (center).

John D. Schapiro with wife, former Eleanor Tydings, at foxhunt

Joseph Cascarella, aide to John Schapiro, at Soviet horse "factory" in Ukraine

Soviet racetrack director (second left) at Laurel (U.S.) Racetrack with Joseph Cascarella and Soviet jockey (extreme right)

Jack Jones Dreyfus, Jr., the "Lion of Wall street"

SEVEN

Sniffing Out
The New-Rich Bourgeoisie

John D. Schapiro, like myself, was born in Baltimore. Like me he is also a Jew. Additionally, his family, like mine, lived in the city's Jewish ghetto, an uncle of his, indeed, having, as a young man, rented a room in my grandfather's tenement house. Both of us, moreover, have been associated with racehorses.

But there is the parallel ends. Schapiro jumped off from his father's junkyard business to marry a beautiful, aristocratic horsewoman, and, through his connection with racehorses, injected himself into the highest circles of the ruling class as a more-or-less tolerated auxiliary member. I, on the other hand, jumped off from my father's burlesque theater business to marry a beautiful, proletarian chorus-girl, and, through my connection with racehorses, infiltrated the highest circles of the ruling class—but merely as a more-or-less tolerated observer.

One such of my infiltrations took place on the occasion of Schapiro's International horse race, which he sponsors annually at his Laurel Race Course just outside of Washington D.C. The race is an event which involves the cream of the international "horsey set" at the very top levels of the ruling class.

The ruling class, especially its "horsey set," being a subject in which both John Schapiro and I have an intense interest, although from opposite poles (his out in the open, mine, of course, always closely concealed) the door was open for me to pursue that interest. As an accredited member of horseracing's press corps, I was permitted to make a documentary film on the 1958 International, a running at Schapiro's Laurel Racetrack which, for the first time, was to see Soviet thoroughbreds participate in an American horse race.

The fact of Soviet participation was of itself, of course, of interest to me. More compelling, however, was my curiosity as to how a Jewish junkman's son went about ingratiating himself into the top strata of the WASP ruling class, and, even stronger, why he would want to.

But first, to fully understand the answers, it was necessary to do some background research.

Morris Schapiro, John's father, I discovered in files of the *Baltimore Sun*, arrived in Baltimore as a Russian immigrant during the Great Baltimore Fire of 1904. He had seventy-five cents to his name. Enough to hire a pushcart. Which he immediately did, and hauled junk metal from the fire's ruins for two cents a load.

Soon he had thirty dollars. Elated with his success at junk collecting, he convinced two immigrant relatives to join him in forming a salvage company, and, with a joint capital of $200, they created the Boston Metals Company, named after the city where he spent his first night in the U.S. In the sixty-five years until his death at eighty-six, Morris Schapiro was one of the world's great scrap-metal kings, specializing in worn-out ships, of which he salvaged more than fifteen hundred. Among his customers, spread from Hong Kong to Genoa, were D.K. Ludwig, one of the world's richest men, and Aristotle Onassis, to whom he sold the Canadian frigate which the Greek tycoon converted into the fabulous yacht, Christina.

Although he did business with such giants of the ruling class, Morris Schapiro made no attempt to crash into their social world. Rather, he seemed content to become a pillar of his local business and religious community. He was a bulwark of Baltimore's Temple Oheb Shalom, on the one hand, and, on the other, a crony of powerful U.S. Senator Millard E. Tydings, for whose re-election campaign he was accused of spending "outrageous sums." He was also a major investor in Maryland's four racetracks, but as far as I could determine, never dreamed, through such connections, of rubbing elbows with racehorse owners like Queen Elizabeth, Winston Churchill, Baron Rothschild, Aly Khan and other exalted personages. That remained for his son John.

A craggy-faced, balding man 5'4" tall, John D. Schapiro goes hatless in all weather, except when horsey-set protocol calls for a hat. Then, at his racetrack, he wears a derby for the ceremony of presenting a trophy to some princess or baron who has won his International. At the foxhunt, John sports a top hat to ride with his horsey-set friends. He compensates for the annoying disparity of his 5'4" height with that of his taller WASP friends by wearing a French custom-made version of a shoe that was once known in less stylish quarters as "Adler Elevators." Otherwise, John Schapiro clothes himself in the most conversative of Savile Row fashions.

"Well, you know," he explains, over a drink in his cozy Laurel Race Track office, "for the last twenty years since I started my International I've been getting over to London regularly. So my tailor has things ready for me. It usually takes three fittings to get a good job, but I manage to do it in two. That gives me time for other shopping. If you have access to markets like these, it's very easy to build your taste around them."

"Speaking of taste," I say, "that ring on your left pinkie finger. Does it have special significance?"

"That? No, it's just a ring I picked up in France. It's bloodstone, my birthstone."

John D. Schapiro, president of Laurel Race Track and impressario of the Washington D.C. International, seems intensely interested in "blood," that is, in exchanging his own for a "bluer" kind. Until the Schapiro family acquired Laurel, however, he manifested little interest in the blueblood horsey set, and, in fact, had never been on a horse, except a childhood pony.

His first marriage, in 1938, was the traditional liason for a promising young man of his background—Jewish girl from a good neighborhood, catered wedding reception at an expensive hotel, religious ceremony in the orthodox tradition. John D. Schapiro, twenty-four, of 907 Lake Drive, Baltimore, married Jeanne Miller, twenty, literally the girl from around the corner, in a June wedding at the Waldorf-Astoria in New York.

After birth of two sons, the marriage fell apart. John, now a free-wheeling bachelor who operated an international junkyard, was president of a racetrack and running around with Maryland's classy Greenspring Valley crowd. He also made connections with the foxhunting elite by joining the Elkridge Hartford Hunt—an organization not especially notable for Jewish membership.

"Sara Secor, the Hunt's joint master, convinced me I should give foxhunting a try. 'We'll just go hill-topping,' she said. 'I'll stay back with you, in case you have trouble.'

'Well, she had me come out on Thanksgiving Day. The meet was at St. James Church, and I showed up in jodphurs and a soft cap. Completely incorrect, of course, but I didn't know any better.

"The field went off from the church and turned into George Constable's place, where we had our first jump. I was on my Irish import. I hadn't taken riding lessons since I was a child. I had told Sara that I didn't know how to jump. But there we were, cantering into the fence. I didn't have any place to go except into it. So that's how I jumped my first fence. My good old Irish hunter simply took care of me."

About this time Schapiro also acquired a townhouse in the city to do the kind of entertaining appropriate to his ever-growing interest in WASP high society.

"I remember when John was being bachelor-stylish around what was then the elegant Mt. Vernon Place area in Baltimore," one of his old acquaintances told me. "He had a classy *pied-a-terre* which featured an immense fireplace that he seemed to think good taste required should never go unused. He'd appear at his parties in riding breeches, and, in the middle of July, light a fire in that damn thing, and then turn up the air-conditioning."

It was during this period of transformation from son of a Jewish immigrant from Temple Oheb Shalom to aspiring foxhunter with the WASPish Elkridge-Hartford Hunt, that John first met Eleanor Tydings (Gillet). She was fair-haired, blue-eyed and 14-karat WASP. She was the daughter of Millard E. Tydings, the U.S. Senator whom his father had supported with "outrageous" campaign funds, and the granddaughter of Joseph E. Davies, ex-Ambassador to Moscow. At her previous wedding, to F. Warrington Gillet, Jr., the guest list included governors, senators, ambassadors and high commissioners—all that kept Supreme Court Chief Justice Vinson away was his premature demise.

It took John about five years and much bumpy fence-jumping to win the fair Eleanor. With this coup he would no longer be embarrassed by having to engage a professional hostess with the right social standing to preside over his fancy promotion parties for his International, such as the 1954 bash for Aly Khan in Saratoga. Now he had at his side his very own Princess of the Royal Blood. The nightmare of being a crass outsider was somewhat relieved, but, having arrived at this dizzying social height, the big question was: How to keep from falling off-balance?

John Schapiro hung doggedly onto his International—his lifeline to the world of "Beautiful People." He thought of his race, as he described it to me, "as being in the same class as the King George VI and Queen Elizabeth Stakes and the Prix de l'Arc de Triomphe." And I, at mention of l'Arc de Triomphe, smiled inwardly at the unconscious comparison of himself with the upstart 5'2" Corsican who managed to grab off, as his second wife, his own Princess of the royal Hapsburg blood. "Indeed," he emphasized, "not only is the International in the same league as the King George, Queen Elizabeth and the Prix, it is also regarded as the race which determines the 'Horse of the World.''

Up until the running of the 1958 International, however, the truth was that few people outside of veteran racegoers had ever heard of the Washington D.C. International. The first two runnings, won by England and France, respectively, had horses only of middling merit, and certainly none owned by great rulingclass names, except that of German Baron von Thyssen. In 1954, Queen Elizabeth II sent a mediocre entry, over the vocal protest of British horse breeding groups, who feared that a bad showing would harm their bloodstock interests in the US—and her horse finished last. The fourth, fifth and sixth runnings saw some improvement. French Comte de Chambure sent a horse in 1955, Sir Winston Churchill (whose entry also ran last) sent one in 1956, and Prince Aly Khan sent one in 1957, with the score standing at two U.S. wins against four by foreign countries. Not much in the way of top horses—not one winner of any of the U.S. Triple Crown races had ever been entered. so far, the "Schapiro Internationale," as one of John's more sardonic critics called it, had been something of a bomb.

But in 1958 John Schapiro managed a coup that immediately put his International not only in column one of the sports pages but on the front page of media throughout the world. That was the year that the Russians came.

Up till then, no Soviet thoroughbred had ever raced this side of what those in the capitalist west, including, of course, Schapiro, likes to call the "Iron Curtain." The vast majority of Americans had no idea that there was even such a thing as horseracing in communist countries (which, incidentally, testifies as to who really closed the Iron Curtain on exchange of information). How could anybody afford to own a thoroughbred under wretched communism? Was there, indeed, something called a "thoroughbred" in the vaunted egalitarian paradise? And betting—is there such a corrupt bourgeois institution as gambling in the proletarian Utopia? John Schapiro sensed the enormous publicity value for his International in lifting the horseracing Iron Curtain to give Americans a glimpse of how "bourgeois decadence" still prevails in the workers Utopia.

However, he didn't personally make the trip to Moscow to

implement arrangements for the Soviet entries, as he always did to London and Paris when soliciting entries from the capitalist countries. Negotiating with the peasants of the USSR Ministry of Agriculture, which oversees Soviet horseracing, was nothing like rubbing elbows with the lords and ladies of the British Jockey Club and the French *Societe d'Encouragement*.

Instead, he sent his brother-in-law, Joseph Cascarella, a one-time professional baseball player turned racing dandy as executive vice-president of Laurel. Nobody had any idea of what the Russian horses and horsemen would look like on arrival in the U.S.

By the time the Soviet plane landed at Baltimore's Friendship Airport that autumn with two Soviet thoroughbreds named Garnir and Zaryad, along with a retinue of trainers, jockeys, grooms and technical personnel, public interest had skyrocketed. Crowds of photographers and reporters came to witness the unloading of the horses. To their surprise, the two Soviet thoroughbreds looked like any other thoroughbred. As for the unfashionable Soviet horsemen, the director of Moscow's Hippodrome racetrack, who had been an aide to Marshall Budenny, the legendary Soviet cavalry chief, wore a three-piece vested suit which, though not as elegant as John Schapiro's hand-tailored Saville Row creations, did his directorial status no disservice. The jockeys, except for their distinctively Russian fur hats, could have walked out of the Belmont Park jockeys room and been mistaken for Eddie Arcaro or Willie Shoemaker. And the trainer, a short, gold-toothed man, might well have been the famous Jewish-American trainer, Hirsch Jacobs. Indeed, his name, suspiciously, was Yevgeni (Eugene) Gottlieb. Later, at the welcoming luncheon, acting like any other naive victim of the rulingclass-inspired myth which holds that *official* anti-Semitism exists in the Soviet Union, I ventured a question in Yiddish. Yevgeni Gottlieb replied:

"Sicher, ich bein Yiddishe. Gottlieb iss ein Yiddishe numen. Feyrde haben nisht anti-Semiten, ihr vayst? Ihr hat Yiddishe feyrde-leyhrners in America, nein? Vus sieht ihr a soy ibbersacht in Russland sennen oyich du feyrdeleyrners?" ("Certainly, I'm Jewish. Gottlieb is a Jewish name. Horses are not anti-Semitic, you know? You have Jewish horse-trainers here in America. Why are you so surprised that there are Jewish horse-trainers in Russia?").

On International Day, November 11, 1958 after jockeys Nicolai Nasibov and Vladimir Kovalev had worked their horses for several days to acquaint them with the track, and trainer Yevgeni Gottlieb and Hippodrome Director Yevgeni Dolmatov had been generously exhibited to the press, the crowds came. Mostly they came to see the two thoroughbreds owned by Soviet Horse Factory No. 33, as the entry was listed in the Laurel program. In the USSR, racehorses are owned, bred, trained and ridden on a communal basis. A collective farm—amusingly translated into English by Laurel's staff as "factory"—owns the horses, and, with trainers, jockeys and stable personnel, communally shares their earnings.

Australia won the 1958 International with Sailor's Guide, the U.S. taking second with Tudor Era, and Ireland third with Ballymoss. Garnir, one of the Soviet horses, did not come off too badly, running sixth, while the other, Zaryad, ran last. The crowds loved it, the media adored it, and John D. Schapiro's International was finally a box-office success.

For the next eight years, except for 1965, the Soviets were

157

there, almost always with two horses. They did better, too, getting a second with a horse named Anilin, and a third with Zabeg. John Schapiro was also doing better, particularly with the aristocracy he pined after. Mrs. Richard C. DuPont now entered Kelso, the world's biggest money-winning horse, along with the plebian Russian "factory" horses. The Aga Khan, Baron Guy de Rothschild, Irish President Eamon de Valera, Jock Whitney and other such rulingclass bigwigs were also coming into the competition.

In 1972, after an absence of five years, the Soviets again accepted a request to enter the race, being, in fact, the first to be invited by Laurel that year. They again submitted their customary two horses: Herold, a colt which had won the Russian Derby, and Skala, a filly of lesser accomplishment.

This was to be Schapiro's most prestigious year. As the season advanced, an acceptance was received from John M. Schiff, U.S. Jockey Club member and international banking mogul. He would be sending down from New York Droll Role, one of the best horses in the country. The sensational Cougar II was coming from California. Riva Ridge, 1972 Kentucky Derby and Belmont Stakes winner, was entered. And, most important, San San, a Prix de l'Arc de Triomphe winner, owned by Countess Margit Batthany, was coming from France. Schapiro was as ecstatic as though he himself had been elevated to the nobility.

Suddenly the picture changed. Schapiro informed the Soviets that he would not accept their second horse, the filly Skala. At that moment the two Soviet horses were already en route to Cologne for trans-shipment to Laurel.

"We could not make them understand that the International was designed for classic horses, not ordinary runners," Schapiro told *Washington Post* reporter, Gerald Strine. "Skala finished fifth in the Grand Prix von Europa in Cologne about a week ago, and we had already turned down the winner of that race, a German horse, Prince Ippi."

"Who is kidding whom and why?" commented reporter Strine.

The Soviets, having invariably sent two horses, retaliated by pulling their Derby winner, Herold, out of the race. John Schapiro had, in effect, erected a Berlin Wall of his own.

Said Shirley Povich, sports editor of the *Washington Post*: "But Schapiro's concept of the International as a race exclusively for classic horses is a brand-new and confounding one. During the previous twenty runnings it has been populated by some of the most hopeless starters ever invited into any race, a fact which suggests that Schapiro's excuse for rejection of the Russian filly—to preserve the integrity of the race—itself deserves rejection.

"In previous years the only excuse for the presence of some foreign horses in the Laurel race was the threatened scarcity of foreign entries. Their embassy connections were also useful, helping Schapiro to flesh out those Upper Turf Club teas he conducts for the odd collections of socialites, positive and putative, in his aerie above the clubhouse."

"Gerald Strine, the *Washington Post's* turf columnist, noted the importance of social connections, when he suggested the other day that the Russian filly might have had her invitation to Laurel were she owned by a czar or a prince, instead of Moscow Horse Factory No. 33."

But this year, 1972, John Schapiro's Upper Turf Club teas were going to be well-packed with Schiffs, duPonts, and various specimens of French, English and American nobility. Who needed Russian peasantry?

For the racing public, however, it was another matter.

"The Russians would have added considerable interest to the race," said Gerald Strine. "They always did. Usually they came in pairs: Garnir and Zaryad in 1958, Garnir and Flang in 1959, Zabeg and Zadorny in 1960, Zabeg and Irtysch in 1961, Zabeg and Liven in 1962, Ivory Tower and Bryansk in 1963."

"Could Skala have been worse than Bryansk? Or Irtysch?"

"Nyet."

"As it is, the International is evolving into a showcase for selling foreign bloodstock, with transportation charges paid in advance. Owners and trainers come here more interested in getting a good price for their horse than in winning the race."

"Meanwhile, rest well in the knowledge that Soviet horses won't squat on Laurel's doorstep in '72. Horse history probably will record that Russian Marshall Kutuzov checked Napoleon's cavalry at Borodino, and Fischer captured Spassky's knights at Reykjavik, but that Schapiro stopped the Russians cold at Cologne."

The twentieth running of the Washington, D.C. International went ahead without the Soviets.

At a West German embassy party in Washington, given to honor Mr. and Mrs. John D. Schapiro two nights before the race, an affair to which I was invited, the two honored guests stood in the receiving line next to Ambassador Rolf Pauls and his wife, smiling and accepting congratulations. The West Germans had been invited to participate in the race and had qualified two horses, the same number, incidentally, as the Soviets had submitted, but, at the last moment, were unable to make it. This, however, in no way dampened enthusiasm for the reception on the part of either the Jewish boy from Temple Oheb Shalom, or for the German Ambassador, an ex-major who had lost an arm fighting Adolph Hitler's war against Jews and Communists.

Said the Ambassador, beaming on the diplomats, socialites, horse breeders and reporters massed at his embassy evening: "Diplomats and horse breeders have much in common. We must both have patience. And we must both know how to pick the moment."

The ex-major of the Nazi Wehrmacht raised his glass in toast to the creator of the Washington, D.C. International and his blueblooded wife, and everyone joined in.

"What a scene!" I couldn't resist saying to the man standing next to me (and at the moment I didn't give a hoot if he was John D. Schapiro's brother-in-law or whoever). "Here's a Jew who considers it an honor to be toasted by a soldier who fought for a man who not so long ago had roasted Jews!"

But the pageant proceeded according to Schapiro's traditional scenario. In the ultra-exclusive Upper Turf Club victory celebration that followed the race, which I also attended, John M. Schiff, as winner of the 1972 International, is being toasted by John D. Schapiro. The self-possessed, 6'2" aristocrat from New York, whose immigrant Jewish grandfather had, like Morris Schapiro, accumulated an American fortune, looks down on the nervous, 5'4" would-be-aristocrat from Baltimore. John Schiff is a partner in the great international banking firm of Kuhn, Loeb & Co., while John Schapiro is but the inheritor of an international junkyard. Both, however, have married into blueblood WASP families. They clink champagne glasses, Mr. Schiff rather impatiently, for his limousine is waiting downstairs to return him to New York. There is just time enough to complete the ceremony.

"You know," John D. Schapiro says to John M. Schiff, raising his glass again. "There is something more we have in common besides horseracing, something dear to both our hearts. Both of us are interested in the Boy Scouts."

EIGHT

Unmasking A Coy Tycoon

It's 1973, and I'm breakfasting with Jack Jones Dreyfus, Jr. in his luxurious Wall Street office. It's the same old story: thoroughbred horses. Thoroughbred racing has always been and still is a hallmark of the ruling class. And Jack Jones Dreyfus, Jr. is definitely, although he likes to play a coy game of maintaining he is not, a functioning member of the ruling class. You don't control a multi-billion-dollar mutual fund called the Dreyfus Fund, which owns huge blocks of multi-national stock, without having your two-cents to say about what goes on in the board rooms of the high and mighty.

Like John Schapiro, Jack Dreyfus is a Jew. Unmistakably a Jew, in fact. For he is related to the renowned 19th century anti-Semitism victim, French army captain, Alfred Dreyfus. Unlike Shapiro, however, he doesn't have to sniff around the thoroughbred WASP establishment offering international horse races in order to wangle invites to their social soirees. Dreyfus is a welcome component of the horsey elite: a trustee of the prestigious New York Racing Association, and a member, along with Whitneys, Vanderbilts and DuPonts, of that "last outpost of U.S. feudalism," The Jockey Club.

So it's not to buy mutual funds that I find myself in Dreyfus' office (even if I wanted to, I've hardly funds to buy paper for the book I'm writing). Instead, I'm there, still in my role of closet red, to talk about his passion for the Sport of Kings.

"How does it feel to be the only Jew in The Jockey Club?" I ask, as I dig into an unkosher serving of bacon and eggs prepared in his office kitchen.

"I don't think of myself as a Jew," replies Jack Jones Dreyfus. "My parents were Jewish. But because your parents have a particular religion doesn't mean you have to adopt it."

"No. But with a forebear such as Captain Dreyfus I should think . . ."

"Not at all," he interrupts. "I don't make religion an issue. I'm not Jewish and I'm not *un*-Jewish, not Catholic or *un*-Catholic. I'm not anything. I simply never adopted a specific religion. Besides, the question of religion never arises in The Jockey Club."

"Could that be because there are no Jews in the Club to raise the issue?"

"John Schiff is a Jew."

"*Was* a Jew. He converted."

"Yes, he did. But, like myself, he had Jewish parents . . ."

"Who left a $140,000,000 estate."

"Mine didn't. My father sold candy canes—those peppermint red and white sticks—out of Montgomery, Alabama. He went up to Louisville one day for the Kentucky Derby and lost all his money. So my uncle, his partner, sent him some samples and told him to work his way back. That's how badly my father loved horses."

"Why, then, if you didn't come from a wealthy family like the rest of The Jockey Club, were you invited to become a member?"

"I'll never know. Because of my good looks maybe," he says coyly.

Despite his diminutive size, Jack Jones Dreyfus is in fact a powerfully attractive man. Dark, slim and wiry, he moves with the grace of a cat. But he has more compelling credentials than mere good looks. At 34, he had been the youngest person to hold a seat on the New York Stock Exchange. Today, at 59 (in the 1973 I'm writing about) he's known as the "Lion of Wall Street," having, with a brash advertising campaign that featured the King of Beasts walking up from the Wall Street subway, built up, almost singlehandedly, a $700,000,000 mutual fund. Along the way, in addition to making millionaires of his friends by buying them into Polaroid stock at five dollars a share and then promoting it to four hundred, he fell in love with a thoroughbred and wound up with a racing stable, one of which trounced the incomparable Secretariat. Now, enormously wealthy but still a Johnny-come-lately to the old horsey establishment, the "Lion of Wall Street" has retired from the stock market. He devotes himself to thoroughbreds and to his medical foundation.

"Some people consider you a snob in reverse," I suggest. "Any truth to that?"

"You mean my watching the races with the Puerto Ricans and blacks in the grandstand instead of from a private box?"

"They say you don't wear a tie and that you look more like an ordinary two-dollar bettor than a Jockey Club member. And that, at bottom, it's only a screen to hide an actual desire to rub elbows with the Whitneys and Vanderbilts."

"Look, I simply believe in being relaxed. There's no symbolism in how I dress or where I watch the races from. I'm in racing to enjoy myself, not to prove anything. And this business

165

of rubbing elbows with the Whitneys and Vanderbilts . . . well, they're nice people to rub elbows with, but that's the furthest thing from my mind."

"What about the time you snapped a woman's picture in Battery Park with a Polaroid camera, and, when she gave you a quarter, you kept it? Or that woman in the Roney Plaza Hotel who thought you were a bellhop, and you kept the tip she gave when you told her where the ladies room was? Weren't those just coy acts to project a self-effacing image?"

"Coy acts? What else could I do? I hate to hurt people's feelings. The woman in Battery Park thought I was a street photographer. She didn't know I was testing the Polaroid for stock promotion purposes. And the other woman simply took me for a bellboy. I just didn't know how to explain that I wasn't what they thought I was."

Sitting with this shy tycoon in his sun-drenched office on the 27th floor of a lower Broadway tower, while the Dow Jones quotations flash on closed circuit TV, I begin to wonder if I've at last encountered a rulingclass figure devoid of those petty vanities which often accompany wealth and power. What actually is this so-called Lion of Wall Street? A bashful Wizard-of-Oz lion? A King-of-Beasts too gentle to crush the mouse at his paw? Or is he, rather, a predatory J.P. Morgan masquerading in Don Quixote costume?

In the corner of the room there's a large antique brass telescope pointing towards Battery Park in the direction of the Statue of Liberty. Is this to provide Morgan-Quixote with the opportunity of keeping sharp vigil over the "Symbol of Freedom" out there on Liberty Island? Or is it for giving a rich do-gooder the chance to spot derelicts in Battery Park who need help, or perhaps stray cats and dogs starving among the ruins of the old Hudson River piers? A fat tabby, a reminder of Dreyfus' feline-oriented days (he's no longer involved with the mutual fund lion or the cheetah which he once used to promote Belmont Park thoroughbred racing) lopes lazily through the room—the only cat, one suspects, that roams about a Wall Street executive suite. Is it one of those rescued strays?

"Jack Dreyfus, despite his shy manner, is said to be a fierce competitor in all he undertakes, whether it be golf, bridge, tennis, Wall Street or horse racing," I remind him. "The implication being that he was always out to demolish his rivals. Particularly in horse racing."

"Not so. I was out to demolish nobody. I couldn't have. I hadn't the resources to compete with any of the racing giants worth toppling. I was fascinated first by the mathematical intricacies of handicapping and betting. Then I fell in love with a filly named Belle Soeur, and, when she was mated with Count Fleet, I was intrigued by the possibilities. I was not well off, but I persuaded Laudy Lawrence to sell me a 25-percent interest in the foal for all I could then afford: 150 shares of Polaroid. (Those shares, incidentally, became worth $234,000 as Polaroid stock skyrocketed).

"The foal was named Beau Gar. He hurt his back and didn't get to the races until he was three, and never had a chance to prove what he could do. I was determined to give that horse a chance. So I bought the rest of him and decided to make him a stallion. Not because of his breeding . . . that's nonsense. You can have the best breeding in the world and have a horse that can't run out of his shadow.

"Then I rented six mares, which is the tail-backward way

of doing things. Usually you own a mare and you rent a stallion. Well, I was incredibly lucky . . . not knowing what a longshot I was playing. In Beau Gar's first crop I got three allowance race winners, a small race winner in Canada . . . *and* Beau Purple!"

He went on to describe, with enormous pride, how his Beau Purple had three times trounced the world's leading money-winning horse, Mrs. Richard DuPont's Kelso. It made me wonder if, after all, the wish to demolish the reigning WASP giants was not indeed the drive that magnetized this relative of Jewish Captain Dreyfus for horse racing. From an obscure Jewish father who peddled peppermint candy canes at the Kentucky Derby to breeding a horse that toppled a DuPont—that is a story to tell your grandchildren! And, at age twenty-two, even as late as 1972, Beau Gar still ranked fourth on the General Stallion List. Jack Jones Dreyfus, Jr.'s Hobeau Farm (the name in key with his self-satirizing style) was now one of the top thoroughbred operations in the country, made even more so by the victory of his Onion (!) over the incomparable Secretariat.

"But racing is not a thing to go into for profit," the Lion of Wall Street warns, summing up his reply to my question about his real motivation. "You could do better in almost any other business. I really don't remember *any* motivation. It was just to give Beau Gar a chance. I was sort of crazy about him."

The pleasantly-fat tabby, which at this moment is sunning itself in the warm rays that filter through Dreyfus' office windows, was, indeed, a homeless kitten he had discovered in Battery Park. Similarly, he'd once spotted through his telescope an abandoned puppy wandering about lower Broadway and rushed down to rescue it. He has since found homes for over fifty homeless dogs and, a while back, seeing fourteen cats cooped up in the lobby of a swank hotel, he immediately arranged to ship them to his 1200-acre Florida horse farm. As I hear from his lips these tales of concern for other living creatures, even though they might be homeless dogs and cats rather than homeless humans, I find myself softening toward this money-grubber. I even begin to speculate whether he would react sympathetically to me, despite discovering that I was his class adversary. Didn't Marx himself, after all, grub money that Engels got from exploiting workers in his textile mill, even though it was used to pursue his mission of rescuing the workers of the world from exploitation by capitalism? *Cats and Dogs of the World Unite*! is, to be sure, a far cry from *Workers of the World Unite*! But it is certainly more admirable than the *nobless oblige* charity and crass concern for self that I've thus far seen with Kennedys, Dukes, Whitneys, et al. Dreyfus' own tabby, as though understanding all this, blinks at the Dow Jones quotations flashing on the TV screen, and his master, pausing a moment over his toast and coffee, blinks along with him.

"Got to keep an eye on the money I don't give away," he says, looking first at the tabby and then at the TV screen, in a kind of apology for the fatness of the pampered animal and the time spent watching stock quotations. "I can't retire completely from the Street, else there'd be no money for my medical foundation."

In 1967, *Life Magazine*, ran a feature story under a banner headline: 10,000-to-1 Payoff. The article was a public confession to reporter Albert Rosenfeld by Jack Jones Dreyfus, Jr., that the macho Lion of Wall Street, had for years been a victim of depression, fear and anxiety. A full-page picture showed the manager of millions in investment dollars cupping his head in his hands, like a man suffering from psychic horrors. An even more sensational *Readers Digest* article followed close upon the *Life* story.

Details of how Dreyfus collected his 10,000-to-1 payoff were even more revealing. After having tried tranquillizers, sleeping pills, psychic energizers, psychotherapy and other treatments to relieve his agony—all to no avail—he came, quite by accident, to what he considered the overwhelming experience of his life: the discovery that he had "too much electricity in his body."

This occurred as a result of touching a vacuum cleaner and getting an electric shock, whereupon he exploded with rage when his wife reminded him that he was always experiencing electric shocks. Consulting with doctors, Dreyfus concluded that an excess of electricity—"hyper-excitable cells," he later explained—was causing his symptoms.

"Maybe," he suggested to his physician, "some people are poisoned by too much electricity, while others have an electrical explosion called epilepsy, which releases it." His hypothesis was a 10,000-to-1 possibility, Dreyfus felt, but just maybe. When his physician informed him that ". . . epileptics *do* have an unusual electric (brain) pattern," the odds fell to 100-to-1 in Dreyfus' mind. And that was the beginning of his experience with the drug called Dyphenolhydantoin (Dilantin), which epileptics take to control seizures.

"It took only a couple of days to lose the need for psycho-therapy," he assures me with a glow in his eyes. "My excessive fear disappeared, and my feelings of impatience, irritability and anger went back to what I view as normal. Instead of getting hooked on a single subject, my mind was able to operate its switch-off mechanism as it should. I could think of things as much as I wanted to, but I could also drop them at will. The neck pains and stomach trouble disappeared. I felt no sedative effect from Dilantin nor any elevating effect. My energy returned full force."

But that was only the beginning. Dreyfus became convinced that not only epilepsy, but also many behaviorial disorders were the result of excess electricity which caused malfunction of the nervous system. He began to take Dilantin regularly and does so to this day.

"I've set up the Dreyfus Medical Foundation for further study of the use of Dilantin in behaviorial disorders . . ."

"Yes, I know," I break in. "I'm very familiar with Dilantin."

"You take it?" he asks smiling broadly, as though he has found a kindred soul.

"My name is Livingston," I remind him. "Doesn't that mean anything to you?"

"Dr. Samuel Livingston of Johns Hopkins Hospital!" he exclaims, leaping from his chair.

My brother was one of the world's leading authorities on epilepsy. As a result of his experience in treating some 15,000 epileptic patients over thirty-five years at his John Hopkins Hospital clinic, he was also a pioneer in the use of Dilantin. And I, having aided in the editing of his several books on epilepsy, had become familiar with the merits and demerits of the drug.

"Why did Dr. Livingston attack me about the *Life* article in his letter to the American Medical Association?" Dreyfus demands.

"As I recall," I reply, "you told *Life* there were no side

effects from Dilantin. But his experience—and you must remember that he's had thirty-five years work with the drug—shows that there are side effects, even deaths. He told me that you had no business practicing medicine in the pages of a mass market magazine, which is how he described your recommendations of Dilantin in *Life*."

"But my medical foundation asked his assistance, and he would have nothing to do with us. I wanted him to contribute his vast experience to our work. Those 15,000 case histories! They could be the answer to how Dilantin affects non-epileptic behaviorial disorders. Couldn't you use your influence to have him cooperate?"

The Ringmaster of the Polaroid Stock Bonanza, Richard Coeur de Lion of the Mutual Fund Crusade, Lion of the Capitalist Money Jungle—and he's asking me, a closet red, to come to his rescue! I'm half-tempted to reveal the hilarious truth of my political orientation.

"My brother is a scientist, Mr. Dreyfus, and you a man with merely an hypothesis. I know nothing about your behaviorial theories concerning Dilantin. How can I pressure him to cooperate when he is so set against your ideas?"

"You've never taken Dilantin?"

"No, why should I? I'm not an epileptic. Besides, I don't blow my fuse when I touch my Electrolux."

"That's not the point. Dilantin can help the normal person. It tunes the mind and body to highest efficiency."

"I'll bet you give Dilantin to your horses to tune them to highest efficiency," I volunteer, smiling.

"There'd be nothing wrong with that," he replies, hedging a direct answer. "The veterinarian may legally prescribe drugs for racehorses, provided they're administered during legal time limits before a race."

"But what about people? Dr. Livingston points to at least twenty deaths associated with Dilantin use."

"That's not our experience. I've taken Dilantin for years and so have others I know of. Last year, in Leningrad, Soviet doctors told me that Dilantin has been widely used there for behaviorial disorders and found extremely successful. Why don't you try it?"

"I don't have any behaviorial disorders" (except, I almost blurt out, this habit of sticking my nose in a world where I don't belong).

"You'd never have to take all those notes you've been taking. Your memory would be better than a computer's. You need to go to the bathroom?"

"No, not really. Why?"

"Well, maybe you do. It's over there in the corner. On the shelf you'll see a glass jar filled with something. If you help yourself I of course know nothing about it."

"You mean you don't want to be accused by another Livingston of practicing medicine," I reply, winking slyly and moving toward the john.

When I come out of the john with a fistful of red-and-white pills, Jack Jones Dreyfus, Jr.'s elfin face lights up like that of an insurance salesman who has just closed a million-dollar policy. I take a Manila envelope with the Dreyfus Fund lion imprinted on it and place the Dilantin inside. Then I shake the Lion of Wall Street's hand.

"You'll try it, I hope," he says. "It's a miracle."

"Oh, sure. One after each meal," I reply, putting the pills

in my case, as he had pocketed the lady's tip at the Roney Plaza.

What else could I do but accept them? Despite his being a member of a ruling class whose trademark, for me, will forever be that newsphoto of a naked little Vietnamese girl running down the road ablaze with U.S. Army napalm (and Dow Chemical is a staple of the Dreyfus Fund portfolio) the man seems a rather gentle and self-effacing soul. He rescues homeless cats and dogs. He worries about people's behaviorial disorders. And I, like he, just hate to hurt people's feelings.

NINE

Dropping In
On David Rockefeller

A Dreyfus and a Duke are one thing, but a Rockefeller
quite another. Tony Duke himself had said that he was "no
Rockefeller that could underwrite a whole nation." And the truth
is that you just don't casually "drop in" to chat with a Rockefeller the way you might with a Duke or a Dreyfus. Especially not
David Rockefeller, who, as the world's Number One banker,
does indeed underwrite whole nations—at a cozy profit, of
course.

Moreover, there's no such thing as a Rockefeller interest in
horses, which might have gotten my foot in the door. In all my
years around the horsey scene, I'd never heard of a Rockefeller
who cared a hoot about horses, except, perhaps, those imaginary
horses that designate the power of the gasoline-consuming
engines which made the Rockefeller fortune.

The power of the press, too, is equally useless for gaining
access to a Rockefeller, although once, in my Acme Newspicture
days, I did manage to sit in on a closed meeting over which John
D., Jr., David's father, presided. I was there for Acme on an
exclusive, as I'd been at the Bankers Trust/Babe Ruth war bond
rally. My assignment was to get a photo of John D., Jr. in his

role of chairman of New York Community Fund (NYCF), a non-profit organization that raised money for local charities.

"Mr. Rockefeller doesn't like posing for publicity pictures," warned the NYCF p.r. man. "So grab him before he slips out. He won't turn you down if you catch him, because he realizes that NYCF is a charity that needs publicity."

Following instructions, I quietly settled in a corner of the meeting room and concealed my camera. The conferring trustees hardly gave me a second look, considering me, I imagine, some insignificant clerk on routine duty.

But my eyes and ears I kept open. Sitting around the conference table was a group of the most powerful members of the U.S. ruling class. I can't recall the names now. Among them, however, were heads of banks and presidents of great corporations who also sat on the boards of banks: Chase Bank, National City Bank, Esso, Mobil, AT&T and others. Nothing less than dozens of billions in capital was concentrated there.

The trustees discussed programs that NYCF would fund in the coming year. Mechanics of budget were debated. There was a bit to-do about priorities. Why, I wondered, were these titans of profit surrendering hours of their valuable time on a non-profit activity? As capitalists, they were no doubt concerned that charity, as Tony Duke pointed out, should go the right way, that is, to help "ward off communism." But perhaps, at bottom, they were also sincerely concerned about the poor. I was still, at the time, a rather naive red, and not quite sure of the answer.

In fact, I was just beginning to feel less guilty about filling up at the Esso station, when John D., Jr. provided me with the answer. (I paraphrase from memory).

"Gentlemen," John D. Jr. announced, after the trustees had raised assenting hands, "we've now approved the NYCF budget of $119-million for the coming year." (I still remember the exact amount—and 119-million 1940s dollars must be the equivalent of at least a half-billion in 1985). "As usual, then, we'll take a loan for that amount to cover operations for the period."

Shades of Bankers Trust handling proceeds of Babe Ruth's war bond rallies until it had realized a profit of one percent! I of course had no idea about what profit Rockefeller's Chase Bank would realize on a loan such as this. But it didn't take much savvy to deduce that these highminded capitalists were surrendering their valuable time to insure that the charity did indeed go the right way, that is, a piece of the loan to each of their respective banks.

For an outsider, particularly a Marxist, eavesdropping on a Rockefeller is a chance that rates odds of 10-million to one. But having a chat with David Rockefeller in the privacy of his office is something that rates even higher odds. So when I decided on "dropping in" to see him, it was like deciding to hitch aboard a rocket to the moon. Nevertheless, I was determined to make a try.

I polish my shoes and put on my three-piece Brooks Brothers business suit. I can't imagine that David Rockefeller, chairman of Chase Manhattan Bank and director of the Federal Reserve Bank of New York, would much relish anybody dropping by in a safari outfit—my regular garb in summertime New York—even if his visitor did look like Dr. Livingstone taking a breather from the jungle.

The public relations department of Chase Manhattan Bank,

however, is a different matter, particularly if you're a writer. Anybody who can scratch out a word is welcome to interview the bank—he could look like Marshall Cinque and represent the Symbionese Liberation Army's *Weekly Times*—who cares, so long as he has a readership. The Great Bank, as its logo: *You Have A Friend At Chase Manhattan*, assures you, desperately desires to be a "friend" to everybody. And I, as I assure Mr. Idan Sims, its p.r. director, am the author of several books. It was through this back door that I hoped to reach David Rockefeller.

"You say you're not interested in figures, annual reports, statistics, that sort of thing?" remarks Mr. Sims, after checking my authorship credentials.

"Only tangentially. It's the *heart* of Chase Bank I want to get at. David Rockefeller is one of the world's most influential men. Certainly he's this nation's most important banker. I'd like a few minutes with him."

"Mr. David is out of town at an International Monetary Fund meeting, so it's obvious you can't see him. Besides, it would require three months notice even if he did consent to receive you. But since you're already here we'll take you through our headquarters building. We'll even let you have a peek at Mr. David's office. Meantime, while I make arrangements, have a look at his bio."

Well, I say to myself, I guess I bit off more than I could chew. But, if I can't have a first-hand crack at Mr. David, at least I'll get an inside look at where the great man works. I start leafing through the official biography Mr. Sims has given me.

David Rockefeller became chairman of Chase Manhattan in 1969, it says. David Rockefeller awarded French Legion of

Honor . . . Mr. Rockefeller receives Honorary Doctor of Law degree from Columbia University . . . Rockefeller, chairman, Council on Foreign Relations . . . David Rockefeller, chairman, Board of Trustees, Rockefeller University . . .

My head swims as I scan the list of sinecures the man had garnered, many of them before he was out of his twenties. You get the feeling that he is an American equivalent of a royal personage—a kind of British Prince Charles, automatically entitled to colonelcies in his country's elite regiments, even while wet behind the ears. Regality is hinted at, too, in the hushed tone with which his p.r. underlings utter the name *Mr.* David, as though they really mean *His Grace, David, Duke of Manhattan.*

"Are you ready," asks Ms. Jo Ann Schaeffer, an attractive young Chase p.r. executive whom Mr. Sims has assigned to shepherd me through the building. "We'll go to the 60th floor first, the Executive Dining Area."

We step into a private elevator filled with a half-dozen of Chase's 150 vice-presidents, who are headed for the upstairs lunchroom.

"Number One Chase Manhattan Plaza was the sixth tallest building in the world when it was erected in 1961," Ms. Schaeffer informs me. "Since then, of course, we've been pushed down the list a bit, with the World Trade towers and the Sears skyscraper in Chicago. But we're still the largest banking operation under one roof. With this building, David Rockefeller changed the course of Wall Street's history."

"How's that?" I ask, as we get out at seventeen and board an express to sixty.

"The banks and big corporations were moving uptown in the 1950s" she replies. "Mr. Rockefeller decided to buck the

179

trend by pouring $137 million into a headquarters building down here in the financial district. This helped stem the exodus and catalyzed the World Trade Center. Lower Manhattan began to change to what it looks like today."

"Didn't Mr. Rockefeller also revamp Morningside Heights, the uptown neighborhood where he attended school as a boy?" I ask. "It's said that he wanted to make the area into his very own, and I quote, 'Acropolis of New York.' "

Ms. Schaeffer nods an enthusiastic assent.

"And in both places, World Trade Center and Morningside Heights," I add, "neighborhood groups protested that he tore down homes of the poor and destroyed small businesses."

"That's right," she concedes. "The complaints were widely publicized by the media. But Mr. David's firmness prevailed. He contended that stores in the World Trade area, for instance, were marginal at best, and that no great city should tolerate marginal operations and marginal areas. Besides, marginal people would never live well, he emphasized, until they could have something better than clerking in seedy stores or dishwashing in sleazy eating places."

This brings to mind, with some sadness, my own experience as a marginal person working for John Diebold in this former marginal district. One of my few pleasures there, along with thousands of other marginal Wall Streeters, was the opportunity to lunch on fresh-shucked oysters, hand-sliced cheeses and home-baked breads at "sleazy" eating places in the wonderful old Washington Market before it was bulldozed for the World Trade Center. But I feel it impolitic to mention this to Ms. Schaeffer, else I might never get to see how Chase officialdom lunches in its private salons atop its non-marginal skyscraper.